Working with Braille:
a study of Braille
as a medium of communication

D1355585

Working with Braille

A study of Braille as a
medium of communication

BARRY HAMPSHIRE

The Unesco Press

Published in 1981 by the United Nations
Educational, Scientific and Cultural Organization
7, place de Fontenoy, 75700 Paris
Printed by Presses Centrales, Lausanne
ISBN 92-3-101864-7

Preface

Unesco's interest in the problems faced by those with some form of handicap is longstanding and has resulted in a number of studies concerning different aspects of special education for the handicapped. Such education aims at preparing handicapped students for a full life in the community.

The severely visually-impaired have specific needs regarding reading and writing, given their dependence on an alphabet composed of embossed dots. As early as 1949 Unesco took the initiative to promote a survey of problems aimed at establishing world Braille uniformity. The Organization asked Sir Clutha Mackenzie of New Zealand to produce a universally acceptable plan for the application of Braille to all languages, thereby fulfilling the hopes of Louis Braille, the blind French professor who invented the alphabet of raised dots for finger-reading in 1829. In 1954, Unesco published the results of this work, *World Braille Usage,* in English, French and Spanish. It was a landmark for the blind of the world and lifted Braille from a jungle of punctographic codes to a universal medium.

There have been developments in this field since then which merit publication, and so Unesco decided to carry out a study on Braille as a medium of communication, dealing with Braille research; the use of Braille; selection, editing and distribution of Braille material; the production of Braille; Braille code systems; and reading, learning and teaching Braille. The study led to this publication, which also deals with presses and Braille libraries, manufacturers of equipment, sources of information relating to Braille, research centres and Braille recorders.

This publication has examined the situation of the visually handicapped in relation to Braille as a medium of communication. It will be of interest not only to persons with a visual impairment but also to teachers, producers of texts in Braille, to anyone closely connected to a person with a visual difficulty and to those interested in the area of communication for and with persons who cannot use their eyes.

The main author and editor of this book is Barry Hampshire (United Kingdom) who is associated with the Swedish Federation of the Visually Handicapped. The late Dr Walter Cohen of the South African National Council for the Blind, Dr Jan-Ingvar Lindström of the Swedish Federation for the Handicapped, and the late John Jarvis of the Royal National Institute for the Blind, United Kingdom, have contributed articles for the book, and numerous experts have in different ways generously contributed to the result of this study.

The Unesco Secretariat expresses its appreciation of Mr Hampshire's work and that of his collaborators. The author is responsible for the choice and the presentation of the facts contained in this book and for the opinions expressed therein, which are not necessarily those of Unesco and do not commit the Organization.

Contents

Acknowledgements

Although the present book is not the co-operative effort originally planned, various organizations and people have contributed significantly towards its completion.

First, I should like to express my gratitude to Unesco for providing the initiative for this publication and to Bengt Lindqvist who, under the auspices of the Swedish Federation of the Visually Handicapped, undertook the responsibility for the work to be carried out.

Secondly, I should like to express my gratitude towards the late Dr Walter Cohen, Jan-Ingvar Lindström, and the late John Jarvis for the articles they contributed.

Furthermore, particular thanks go to Dr Jeanne Kenmore of Helen Keller International, who provided material relating to the Braille presses and libraries, and the sample problems in the Braille mathematics codes and to Anders Arnör who not only read and commented on all the chapters as they were written, but also encouraged and supported the work from beginning to end.

I should also like to thank the following people who read and commented upon the manuscript in preliminary form: Ms Ulla Cahling, Dr J.M. Gill, Dr J. Kenmore, Dr H.-J. Küppers, Mr B. Lindqvist, Mr W. Poole and Dr M. J. Tobin. In no way, however, should these readers be held responsible for any errors that may remain.

Finally, I should like to express my gratitude to Ms Elaine Bryant for her patience and skill in transforming my preliminary draft into a presentable manuscript in such a short time.

B.H.
Stockholm
March 1979

Introduction

Braille has been the major medium of communication for the severely visually handicapped for more than a century. It has been adapted to all the major languages of the world and most of the minor ones. Furthermore, special Braille code systems have been worked out to represent mathematics, scientific symbols, music, phonetics and other specialized symbol systems.

Braille has, thus, proved flexible when faced with the problem of creating a new code system out of the fixed-character set of just sixty-three characters. In fact, this flexibility coupled with the many enthusiastic and inventive Braille experts in several countries, has proved to be a weakness of the system. This is because many countries have arrived at different Braille code systems for the same print symbol system, which sadly has resulted in nearly a dozen different Braille mathematics codes, at least two different ways of disposing Braille music, and half a dozen different Braille computer codes, etc.

In the early 1950s Unesco, together with other international organizations, such as the World Braille Council and later the World Council for the Welfare of the Blind (WCWB), attempted to achieve some standardization of the various Braille codes. In 1954, Unesco published *World Braille Usage* which presented charts of the Braille codes of all the languages which had one. Since 1954, WCWB has tried to continue this work of standardization through its various subcommittees, although with limited success.

During the nearly thirty years since the publication of *World Braille Usage* a great many changes and developments—socially, technologically, economically—have occurred in most societies and these have had significant implications for communication media for the visually handicapped.

For example, the increased wealth of many countries has allowed considerable expansion in the use of such alternative media as talking books and special low-vision aids. The general expansion of research and development activities, especially during the 1960s and early 1970s, has resulted in increased effectiveness of Braille production techniques and greater insight into the Braille reading process. The current trend towards automation has meant that the visually handicapped require much more effective access to information in order to compete for jobs, as these increasingly demand the handling of information in some way or another. In short, the demands on Braille have become more exacting. It must be available quickly as people are no longer prepared to wait several months for a book. It must reach a wider range of people as authorities and organizations can no longer afford to pay for it when alternative media, although perhaps less satisfactory in some cases, can be produced more cheaply and reach a much greater number of the blind and visually handicapped.

The major problem with Braille today is, therefore, no longer standardization. Although desirable, this seems to be something everyone must live without, at least for the foreseeable future. What is important is the dissemination of the information which is currently available about Braille to as wide an audience of practitioners, administrators, teachers, social workers and, not least, to Braille readers themselves, as possible. Much of this information is only disseminated through academic publications and, therefore, often does not reach the kind of people who could make most use of it.

The purpose of this book is, then, to provide a source for information about the developments relating to Braille which have taken place during the past thirty years.

Chapter 1 discusses the use of Braille and its relationship to other media such as talking books, large-print books and reading machines. There have been such significant developments in the production and distribution of these media that they have often been discussed in terms of threatening the continuing use of Braille. There seems little chance of any of these alternatives providing any total substitute for Braille. On the other hand, these alternatives are useful for certain types of material in certain situations. The optimum areas of use of Braille, in relation to other media, are then important to define if visually handicapped people are to gain the maximum benefit from each.

The two following chapters are concerned with Braille production. This involves a process starting with selection of material for publication in Braille, editing the material so that it is appropriate for the medium of Braille, the actual production of the material and finally its distribution. The actual process used for the manufacture of Braille underwent considerable development during the 1960s and 1970s and these are presented in Chapter 3. The other aspects are presented in Chapter 2.

One of these aspects—editing—is of particular importance as it is usually forgotten in any discussion of Braille production process. The layout of material in a Braille book is of great importance to its readability, especially when tables or illustrations are involved. The limitations of the tactile sense must constantly be borne in mind as a direct transfer of a print book to tactile form is rarely possible.

Chapter 4 takes up the problem of Braille code systems. It has not been the purpose of this chapter to present any detailed description of international usage. With respect to literary codes and some special codes, such as the phonetic code, a detailed presentation will be given in the revised edition of *World Braille Usage* which Unesco hopes to publish in the early 1980s. A brief overview of developments in literary, mathematics and music codes since the 1950s is given, together with some illustrations of how some of the various existing mathematics and music codes differ.

This is a very specialist area and a more detailed treatment would be out of place in the present book.

Chapter 5 reviews the research which has taken place on reading, learning and teaching Braille. This is the only area, other than the technological one, that has received a significant amount of research. Despite this concentration of research, there are still a number of needs and problems remaining in these areas. These are discussed in Chapter 6. Also, additional areas which so far have received little or no research, yet nevertheless warrant investigative studies, are described in this chapter.

Each chapter, with notes and references, is complete in itself. There are also five appendices which give names and addresses of Braille printing houses and libraries, manufacturers of equipment which produce or in some other way relate to Braille, sources of information, research centres and finally one dealing with Braille recorders. The latter are equipment which have only recently become available. They are potentially relevant to nearly every chapter in this book, although they are still too recent to be able to give any meaningful evaluation of just how big their impact will be.

Although many readers may only be interested in certain chapters of this book, and, as stated above, each is quite independent, there are nevertheless many inter-relationships between the different aspects treated by each chapter. The pattern of Braille use, for example, has obvious implications for developing new Braille production facilities. Similarly, inadequacies in Braille editing and layout may be creating problems for learners of Braille. It is hoped, therefore, that readers will be tempted to at least read quickly through the whole book, even if only a single chapter is read thoroughly.

Chapter 1

The use of
Braille

Factors affecting
Braille usage

Visually handicapped persons form a minority group within the general population.[1]
Braille readers within the visually handicapped population also form a minority
(usually estimated as between 10–15 per cent in Western Europe and North America).
However, the actual number of people who actually use Braille *regularly* is even
smaller and could be as low as 0.5 per cent of the visually handicapped population
even in countries where there are well established Braille production facilities.

The use of figures in this context, however, perhaps gives a misleading indication
that it is possible to quantify these populations with some degree of confidence—it
isn't. Consider a study carried out by the European Regional Council (ERC) of WCWB
on the activities of Braille printing shops and libraries which states 'it should be
pointed out from the start that it is hardly possible to establish relations between the
number of inhabitants of a country in general... and the number of blind'.[2] For
example, the survey showed that the Federal Republic of Germany and the United
Kingdom of Great Britain and Northern Ireland had approximately 58.5 million and
55.5 million inhabitants respectively, yet the former reported only 60,000 blind
against the latter's 116,000.

There is not, of course, an incidence rate of visual handicap nearly twice as high in
the United Kingdom as in the Federal Republic of Germany. The explanation of these
figures lies in the definition of blindness, or rather, the lack of agreement between
definitions of blindness employed in different countries. Difficulties of a similar nature
also prohibit any international comparisons between the use of Braille. Thus, statistics
concerning the visually handicapped and their sub-populations, such as Braille
readers, should be treated with great caution.

It can be stated fairly reliably, however, that Braille reading is carried out by a
relatively small proportion of the visually handicapped population, even if one
considers only those with very severe visual impairment. This naturally prompts the
question—Why? From studies carried out on the use of Braille, three main aspects

can be suggested as contributing to this situation. These are: (a) population characteristics; (b) inherent difficulties of Braille; and (c) use of alternative media.

Population characteristics

Before describing some specific characteristics of the visually handicapped population that are directly relevant to the use of Braille, it will be useful to note how visually handicapped populations are estimated. Once the study population is located, which can often be difficult, there are essentially two approaches: an objective test of visual acuity using the Snellen chart or equivalent,[3] or the use of a 'check list' relating to functional characteristics.[4] The former has the advantage of being administratively straightforward but there are, however, inadequacies in using such a definition derived from this procedure. Use of a functional classification is administratively an enormous task and practically difficult to carry out and standardize on a large scale. This approach does have the advantage, however, of being more relevant and useful to educators, rehabilitation experts, mobility officers, or other such persons professionally involved with the blind.

We will now consider two features of the visually handicapped population that have a direct relevance to the use of Braille. These are age and residual vision.

Age

The age structure of the visually handicapped population is quite different from that of the general population. In the United States of America and many other developed countries it forms almost the mirror image of the general population (see Fig. 1).

This structure is probably different for many developing countries where children form a much larger part of the general population. Futhermore, certain countries have a particular high incidence of visual handicap due to local diseases that cause blindness. The pattern illustrated by Figure 1, however, represents the likely base pattern of blindness, and therefore, the likely pattern of all countries when, or if, blindness prevention and other aid programmes of a more general nature are successful.

It is also worth noting that some countries, such as Sweden, show a different structure in their general population. That is to say, it is becoming more similar to that of the visually handicapped population, i.e. dominated by elderly people.

Taking the structure illustrated in Figure 1, those under 25 comprise nearly half the general population, whereas those of 65 plus account for a very small proportion indeed. On the other hand, 65 per cent of the visually handicapped population are 65 or older and only 4 per cent are under 25. The main reason for this is simply that 'getting old' is often accompanied by failing eyesight.

In a detailed survey of the reading and mobility habits of the 100,000 registered blind in England and Wales in 1965,[5] age of onset of visual handicap was found to be a significant factor in learning to read Braille. Their study showed that only 3 per cent of those who became visually handicapped after they were 60 years old became good enough to read Braille books, compared to 72 per cent of those who were visually handicapped from birth. Furthermore, this survey suggested that age of onset is related to the learning of Braille also. It was found that '90% of those who learned Braille at school said they became good enough to read a book, whereas only 43% of those who had learned Braille but not at school, claimed to have got good enough to read a book'.[6]

It is also reported by Schauder and Cram[7] that

at the National Seminar on the Library Needs and Study Problems of Visually Handicapped Students in South Africa the contributions of blind participants made it clear that within the student group it is usually only those who have been blind from birth or early childhood who are truly at home with Braille as a study medium.

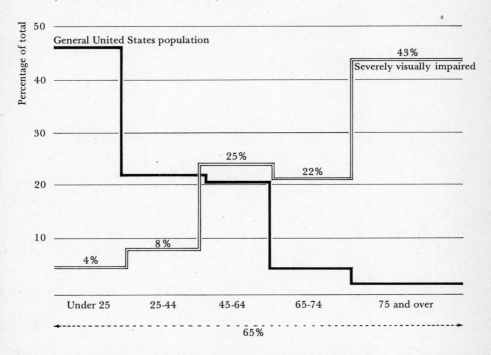

Fig. 1. Estimated age distribution of population with visual acuity of 20/200 or less with usual correction. (After L. H. Goldish, 'The Severely Visually Impaired Population as a Market for Sensory Aids and Services', *The New Outlook,* June 1972, p. 186.)

These comments reflect, however, the existing state of affairs with regard to age and Braille readership. This does not necessarily reflect what is possible. In this context, therefore, it is interesting to contrast a finding of Tobin's:[8] 'It would seem that age as such was not a very important variable in the learning of Braille, at least in the sense that there was no significant correlation between it and Braille reading performance.' It should be noted, however, that there were no very young learners in the group, thereby reducing the possibility of any age-dependency being shown in the results.

Residual vision

The term 'residual vision' is another global expression which cannot be interpreted simply. A detailed visual field estimation can be important for choice of media, as, for example, with homonymous hemianopia, a condition in which half of the visual field is blind. If the left half is missing this does not affect learning to read print very significantly because scanning ahead of the word being read can be done with the remaining right half of the visual field. With right-sided hemianopia, however, this cannot be done so easily and consequently learning to read will be made much more difficult.[9] Such diagnostic details may be important when deciding whether someone should learn to read print or Braille.

From the survey by Gray and Todd, it appeared that the amount of residual vision had relatively little relation to whether Braille was learnt. Their findings are illustrated in Table 1.

Table 1.   Whether the blind person is a Braille reader by the survey classification of residual sight useful for reading print (percentage)

Whether the blind person is a Braille reader	Aged 16-64					
	Cannot see windows	Can see windows but no more	Can see more but did not read large print	Did read large print but not generally ordinary print	Did read large print and does generally read ordinary print	All
Never learned Braille	16	35	40	41	37	33
Learned but not good enough to read	26	29	28	27	26	27
Learned and got good enough to read	58	36	32	32	37	40
	100	100	100	100	100	100
Base	271	176	344	135	110	1,044 [1]

1. These totals include cases for which the sight classification was unknown.
Source: Table 10.6 in Gray and Todd, op. cit.

Apart from the group who could not see the light from windows, the results show little variation in the distribution of Braille readers with their residual sight.

These findings, however, should be contrasted with two studies carried out in the United States[10] that found quite the opposite pattern. These studies were carried out using children who were enrolled in residential and local school programmes. They were categorized into nine 'vision levels' ranging from 20/200 to totally blind. In both studies, it was found that 'the degree of residual vision related to the reading medium: the greater the remaining vision the greater the tendency to read print and the less the remaining vision the greater the tendency to read Braille'.[11]

The explanation of the differences between the American findings and those in the United Kingdom can also be found in Nolan's paper.[11] He found a general decrease of 5 per cent in the proportion of students reading Braille and a corresponding 5 per cent increase in the proportion using large print over the two-year period between 1961 and 1963. Furthermore, for students attending residential schools a shift towards reading large print ranging from 12 to 32 per cent was revealed in six out of the nine visual categories. This change undoubtedly reflects a change in policy on behalf of the residential schools. As Nolan states, 'it is encouraging to see evidence of a strong tendency in the residential school towards making a more realistic match between degree of vision and reading medium. No doubt many factors have been influential in stimulating this shift. Among these are undoubtedly the influence of the 1961 report, greater knowledge and emphasis on visual efficiency, use of vision and optical aids and greater stress on adequate individual diagnosis and treatment.'[11]

This trend towards utilizing residual vision was later coming to the United Kingdom, and the non-relation between residual vision and mode of reading found by the Gray and Todd survey probably reflects the educational policy then followed in that country.[12] This view on maximum use of residual vision has now become fairly widely accepted in Western countries; the Union of Soviet Socialist Republics, however, has not, as it favours the view that overuse of residual vision can damage sight further.[13]

Inherent difficulties in using Braille

It is becoming more accepted that reading, as a skill in general, is not naturally acquired by everyone. With improved monitoring of educational standards a surprisingly high level of illiteracy has been found, even among the most advanced nations. If, then, a reading medium had difficulties inherent in its nature, then learning to use this medium can indeed be expected to demand a relatively high level of motivation, effort and aptitude.

Difficulties in learning Braille

One testimony to the difficulty of learning Braille emerged from a British survey[14] of reading ability among 10- to 16-year-old visually handicapped children who were being taught Braille: 40 per cent of the children were not sufficiently proficient to even attempt the test!

One difficulty of Braille, which hinders its more widespread use to a great extent, is that it is difficult to perceive, at least in the early stages of learning. This will, of course, be related to age and circumstances during the onset of the handicap. Most people, who have reasonable vision, rarely use their tactile sense for detailed discrimination. Thus, to find oneself dependent on this 'unusual' sense takes some time to adjust to. However, it must be emphasized that the perception of Braille characters is well within the capabilities of our tactile senses (assuming that they are not hampered by such things as callouses or scars on the fingers, or additional handicaps that prevent co-ordinated movement of the hands).

Perhaps a more important factor, inasmuch as it can be altered, is the difficulty of the code systems used by some countries. The effects of contractions on Braille reading will be taken up in Chapter 5. It will suffice here to quote the psychologist Paul Kolers, speaking at a seminar on blindness research:

If the set of marks we use for reading is such as to require extended intellectual effort for their perception, as seems to be the case with Braille, substantially less of our cognitive resources will be available for making contact with our stores of information, for interpreting or thinking about the information we are perceiving.[15]

Availability

An obviously discouraging factor inhibiting the more widespread use of Braille is its availability, or perhaps more accurately, the lack of it. To learn Braille, even to someone of above average ability, represents a considerable commitment, in terms of time and effort, on the part of the learner. This will be especially true for those who have been used to reading print, and may be regarded as not worth the effort by someone whose only requirement is light reading for relaxation.

Another factor relevant here is whether there are courses available for adults to learn Braille, especially full-time courses where Braille can be studied intensively under guidance. Teach-yourself Braille manuals are available,[16] although maintaining motivation to learn Braille, if learning alone, can be a difficult problem.

Nature of Braille

A further factor influencing a person's decision to learn Braille may be the nature of Braille itself. Braille is not a neutral carrier of information in the way that most people would regard print. A person using Braille is also implicitly acknowledging a severe degree of visual handicap—the condition of 'blindness' and all this entails psychologically and sociologically. As Graham[17] points out, it is these social factors which probably account to a large extent for the discrepancy between estimates of visual handicapped populations using objective measures and those using functional classifications.[18]

It is also probably true to some extent that Braille reading populations may reflect people's attitude towards their handicap as well as their lack of sight.

Use of alternative media

Although Braille is by far the most well-known means of communication and information exchange used by the visually handicapped, it is by no means the exclusive one. Other media that are now becoming commonly used by the visually handicapped include large print, tape and cassette recorders, and a variety of sensory aids. The increasing use of these alternatives has naturally affected the amount of use made of Braille; some people have even suggested that Braille does not have much future and will eventually be replaced by some or all of these alternative aids and materials.

Although there seems little evidence for Braille becoming completely obsolete, its continuing use must be seen in the light of these new developments, which may be more useful for certain specific purposes or types of material than Braille. It will be useful, therefore, to discuss briefly each of the above types of communication aid with the aim of trying to delimit their range of usefulness, availability, advantages and disadvantages, etc., thereby developing a clearer idea of the areas where development of Braille should be concentrated.

Large print

The use of large print for reading by the visually handicapped has been increasingly encouraged since the ophthalmologic doctrine of 'saving sight' was replaced by one of 'utilizing residual vision' to the maximum extent.[19]

Facilities for producing large print have lagged behind demand, perhaps mainly because the section of the visually handicapped population who have most need of this provision—the partially sighted—have only relatively recently been recognized as a group requiring special aid.

In addition to books actually published as 'large-print books', there is also the possibility of enlarging existing print material. Numerous photocopying machines are now available that can do this. The only condition is that the print must be of good quality since enlargement shows up the flaws in print quite markedly, even at quite low levels of magnification.

In fact, size of type is only one of a number of factors that influence the readability of type, none of which are straightforward. For example, the normal ageing process results in (eventual) presbyopia (i.e. the eye can no longer focus clearly on very near objects). This is commonly manifested in adults increasingly having to hold objects further away in order to get sharp focus; this process, however, also reduces the size of the image on the retina. A study has shown that partially sighted children (who generally retain their power of accommodation despite one or more eye diseases) are able to enlarge the image for themselves by bringing the object close to the eyes.[20] This means that virtually all the children studied, despite being educated in special schools (61 per cent had distance vision of 6/36), were able to see normal 12 point print when they were not restricted to the normal reading distance of about 14 inches. This was not the case with adults because of their decreasing power of accommodation. An implication of this finding is that increasing use and availability of large print may well have differential effects across the age groups of Braille readers. That is, it is likely that far more children (i.e. children with a greater range of visual defects) are likely to be able to benefit from large print, whereas adults, with increasing presbyopia, would find large print an increasingly difficult medium, and Braille might be a more beneficial long-term solution in some cases.

Tape and cassette recorders

The introduction of recorded books (originally on either open reel tape or discs) from the 1930s onwards has had a major impact on the use of Braille, especially in the area of casual reading matter. With the introduction of portable cassette players/recorders the effects became more widespread, as these could be used for note-taking in lectures and classes, for memoranda and personal letters, as well as for listening to pre-recorded material. In fact, this aid has perhaps come closest to challenging Braille as both a reading and *writing* medium.

Cassette recorders are now essential pieces of equipment for students, visually handicapped people employed in occupations requiring the taking of notes, and also for many visually handicapped people generally for everyday note-taking of such items as addresses, telephone numbers and personal memoranda. In fact, many students do not recommend Braille for note-taking[21] because of the slowness of writing it and the need for a lot of working-up afterwards, although it is preferred generally to recorders for short notes, indexing, spelling and translation.

The precise effect of pre-recorded 'talking books' depends on the situation within each country. In Sweden, the introduction of pre-recorded magazines and newspapers, as well as books, during the late fifties and early sixties resulted in a considerable drop in Braille reading. In the United Kingdom, on the other hand, the development of talking newspapers and magazines has been much slower, although talking books are now used fairly extensively. As a result, the effects on Braille readership have been much less than in Sweden. This again[22] reflects the influence of policy decisions on the use of reading media for the visually handicapped.

Sensory aids

This is another rather ill-defined term. In its most general sense, it is an aid which converts information which is normally received by one sense to a form which can be received by another sense. With regard to the visually handicapped, it usually has a more restricted usage; aids 'to permit access to printed matter and to permit safe travel through the environment'.[23] We shall only be concerned with those aids which relate to gaining access to printed matter, which can, for our purposes here, be best discussed under two headings: 'Closed Circuit Television Systems' and 'Direct Access Reading Machines'.

Closed-circuit television (CCTV) systems. These systems provide for large-print readers the equivalent service that direct-access reading machines provide to Braille readers (see page 21). Their use, however, is relevant to a certain extent to our consideration of the use of Braille. This is because CCTV presentation has the flexibility to provide the optimum form of print, in terms of magnification, illumination, contrast, etc., to suit the reader's residual vision. In other words, its widespread use could further reduce the overall population which has so little sight that their vision is completely non-functional. The following description by Genensky shows the possible extent of this reduction.

A 43 year old woman . . . began losing her eyesight from glaucoma when she was 19. This woman's left eye has been enucleated and the visual acuity in her right eye is zero. She does, however, possess some light projection capability in her right eye. She can see bands of light and dark if fingers are back lighted and held an inch away from her right eye. She cannot resolve even the semblance of fingers if they are front lighted. . . . I presented this woman with printed material containing many type sizes and lighted in a variety of ways and at various intensities and found that she could not read any of the material with or without optical aids. With the help of our closed circuit TV systems, however, she was able to read typewriter type magnified four times at the rate of about 100 words per minute, and to write and draw with a felt pen.[24]

It is difficult to say how typical the above case is, but it must, in any case, be balanced by factors such as cost and availability. In Sweden, for example, people requiring sensory aids for vocational purposes are given a substantial grant to buy them, and in the Federal Republic of Germany, for example, every visually handicapped person receives a monthly grant that can be used towards buying such aids. In many countries, however, few visually handicapped people are in a position to buy such aids, or have them bought for them. Furthermore, many potential users may not be prepared to put up with the low reading speeds that would be implicit if they required large magnification; if their residual vision was not particularly suited to visual reading, they might prefer to read Braille instead.

The effects of CCTV on the use of Braille, then, are likely to be complex, and specific to each country. However, their use is likely to increase, especially if their costs go down, and many CCTV users may well have been Braille users before CCTV became available.

Direct-access reading machines. The principle of direct-access reading machines for the visually handicapped is that they 'read' material which is printed or written, and then convert this input into a form which, when displayed, can be perceived by a blind person. The development of such machines is currently undergoing considerable technological advances, and these developments are reviewed in the following section by Jan-Ingvar Lindström of the Swedish Institute for the Handicapped.

Technological advancements of reading machines

Despite being a very important reading medium, Braille has always had a great drawback; the inkprint material to be read has to be processed in order to become available for the visually handicapped person. Therefore, the ideal to many blind people would be a reading machine, which is able to accept any print or handwritten material and present it, for instance, as spoken information. Much effort has been put into the task of developing reading machines, although for decades very little has become useful to the visually handicapped population.

Reading machines, i.e. machines that can 'see' printed or handwritten letters and convert them into a non-visual form can be said to consist of three parts: an information collecting unit or detector, a signal processing unit, and a display unit. From the functional point of view, it is also appropriate to divide them into two groups, namely direct translating machines and character-recognizing machines (Fig. 2).

As the name suggests the direct translating machines transform the visual information into

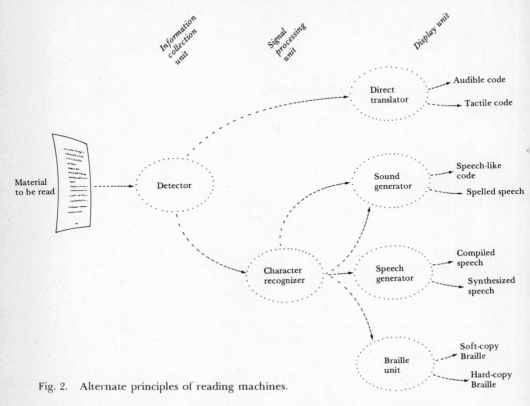

Fig. 2. Alternate principles of reading machines.

some other code, audible or tactual, while the interpretation of the code is left to the user. The character-recognizing machines, on the other hand, as well as incorporating logic for pattern recognition, are also capable of identifying the symbols read. Thus, speech, as well as Braille, are possible as outputs from character-recognizing machines.

One class of direct translating reading machines includes those dependent on even scanning of the print, i.e. a temporal factor (motion) is necessary for the interpretation. Most classic reading machines, e.g. the Optophone, the Batelle device, the Visotoner and later the Stereotoner follow this principle. Figure 3 illustrates the idea.

The print to be read is scanned by a camera, which can be moved along the lines, which contains an array of light sensitive photocells on which a narrow segment of the letter is projected. Every cell controls a tone generator, and so reading is done by listening to a 'melody' which is specific for every letter.

Although the auditory sense has a temporal character, it has not been found easy to read very quickly with these kinds of machine (rarely more than 30 words per minute). This is very low, even compared to Braille reading, where 90 words per minute is not unusual, and of course sighted reading where several hundred words per minute can be reached.

Another class of direct translating machine includes those not exclusively dependent on motion for interpretation, but more probably on a combination of temporal and spatial features. The principle of such machines is illustrated in Figure 4.

The images of the letters are projected on to a two-dimensional array (matrix) of photocells. Those cells which are blocked out from light by the dark letter actuate corresponding tactile stimulators, normally in a matrix of axially vibrating pins. Thus a vibrating relief of the letter is

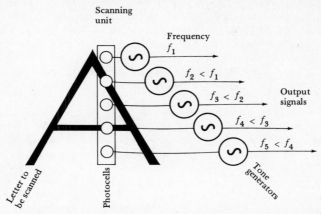

Fig. 3. Principle of the kind of direct translating reading machines, where scanning is necessary for the interpretation of a symbol.

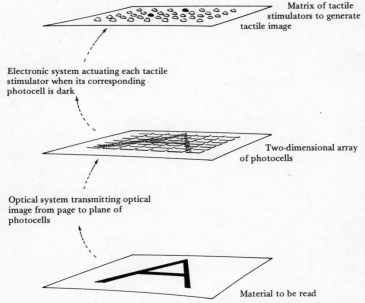

Fig. 4. Principle of image conversion in a direct translating reading machine where scanning is not necessary for the interpretation of a symbol.

created that can be touched by the fingertips (or by a large skin area, e.g. the back or abdomen) and interpreted. The most well-known example of this type of machine is the Optacon, where reading speeds up to 80 words per minute have been reported, although half this speed is supposed to be more typical. Almost 5,000 Optacons have now been distributed over the world, and training programmes are available in several different countries.

In order to reach higher reading speeds the output form has to be better matched to the human information processing capacity. Speech and Braille output are reasonable approaches. Only character-recognizing machines can be considered in this context because the print letters must be recognized before they can be converted to an alternative form. Such alternative forms can range from speech sounds to fully synthesized speech, an output form which does not need to be learnt in order to be understood. Machines of this kind are now being developed (e.g. the character-recognizing Optacon) and are even in production (e.g. the Kurzweil reading machine). A machine with a hard-copy Braille output has also been developed (e.g. the Texto-Braille). Some experience has now been gained from these kinds of machines, and the results are not uninteresting.

From the technical point of view there are many good reasons for an optimistic view of the development of character-recognizing reading machines. Researchers are successfully working with the development of versatile character recognizers, and the knowledge of how to generate acceptable human-like synthetic speech has already resulted in commercially available speech generators. However, it must be considered a much more difficult task to introduce a character-recognizing reading machine, with synthetic speech output, than it is to introduce other advanced technical aids. For example, modifications must be made for every language, thus highly qualified linguists/technicians must be involved in most countries. There are also some difficulties to be considered. One is that much literature is of a very complex nature. Consider, for example, newspapers with a large variety of fonts and lay-outs, scientific literature, where often diagrams, tables, equations and pictures are mixed with the text. How will the machines handle that material? Another question deals with the reader's reading speed and endurance. Where are the acceptable limits? Also, which categories of visually handicapped persons will be able to utilize the new technique? What will the introduction of reading machines mean in the long run to the use of Braille and producing Braille material? In what situations is synthetic speech output an acceptable substitute for a human voice in talking book materials? And the price: What benefit is necessary, or should at least be expected, for the investment?

There are no answers to these questions today, but hopefully the next five years will show up the reaction from the consumer groups, as well as society in general, with regard to the usefulness of these new aids.

The above discussion of alternative media for the visually handicapped illustrates that Braille is in no danger of being replaced, or being made obsolete. It does appear, however, that ordinary light or casual reading does have a genuine alternative in recorded material judging from the effects the introduction of this medium has had on Braille use in some countries. At the same time, many readers may *prefer* to read Braille to listening to a talking book, an essentially passive process. Most of the devices have the effect of extending the range and areas of functioning of the visually handicapped, and do not represent any threat to the continuing existence of Braille.

Classification of Braille usage

This chapter has so far been concerned with factors influencing the use of Braille. In order to obtain a more usable picture of Braille use, however, some consideration of the different types of readers should be presented.

In an analysis by Goldish of Braille use in the United States, the different types of reader were classified as follows: school children, students, employed blind, casual readers, aged blind and deaf-blind.[25] This seems to be a useful classification, so each of these groups will now be briefly discussed.

School children

Of the groups described here, requirements for school children are probably the best documented. However, even with the relatively detailed statistics on school children, there are still many difficulties in obtaining a detailed and reliable picture of needs.

It appears, however, that in most developed countries there is little evidence that new registrations of visually handicapped babies will decline much below the present levels. The reason for this is that, in the foreseeable future, childhood blindness will be largely the

result of irremediable congenital and hereditary disorders. Things may actually get worse, for recent years have seen the emergence of new causes of infantile blindness of which retrolental fibroplasia is only an extreme example. [Furthermore] better management of premature infants and of infants requiring special care is keeping alive a group of babies who show substantial incidence of multiple defects, of which blindness is only one.[26]

It would appear, therefore, that the numbers of visually handicapped children in most developed countries are likely to remain fairly constant in the immediate future, and that numbers in those developing countries where the incidence of childhood visual handicap is still high will hopefully decrease towards this level as health-care programmes begin to be effective. Requirements for materials, however, are not likely to follow this trend. The dominating characteristic of the Braille material required at school is the range of types of material that is used. These range from full-length and often complex (from a Braille point of view) textbooks to short notes, requiring special formatting, illustrations, diagrams, etc., in some cases and the simplest prose in others.

This range of material is likely to be greatest in countries with integrated education, as the visually handicapped pupils' texts and materials will need to reflect as accurately and comprehensively as possible the texts of their sighted peers. However, the different nature of tactile and visual perception would need to be kept strongly in mind so that the visually handicapped pupil was not put at a disadvantage by being presented with simple-minded, 'tactile analogues' of the print material. (See Chapter 3 for a more detailed discussion of this.)

A further important characteristic of school material, and this will be especially true in integrated contexts, is the lack of uniformity and continuity of use of textbooks. Thus, some books may only be in use for one or two years before a school may change to a more recently published book or to one they feel superior; naturally, any visually handicapped pupils would also require these new books to be available to them.

Students

This group, although representing the numerically smallest group, has perhaps the most urgent and difficult needs for Braille material for a production system to meet. It will, almost exclusively, involve meeting individual needs which may often be irregular, and also sometimes urgent. To a certain extent, however, a proportion of the student's likely needs can be obtained from reading lists which (in some cases) are available several months in advance of a particular course beginning. Frequently, however, these are rather general and it may not become clear until the student actually begins the course which particular books are essential and which are just background reading.

One advantage of books at this level is that they will, to some extent, have lasting value. Often, there are classic textbooks in a particular field that successive students will need to use over many years. It is perhaps rather fortunate that this is the case as such books are often very difficult and time consuming to produce, and it is probable that there will be only one or two transcribers in a particular country with sufficient skill and experience to do such transcription. Furthermore, at the present time it is just these kinds of books that present the greatest difficulty to any kind of automated Braille production.

Employed blind

Relative to the sighted population, the visually handicapped are concentrated into only a few occupations—167 compared to 1,506 occupations represented by the sighted. These totals are across twenty-one countries in Europe; the numbers of occupations represented by the visually handicapped in any one country is less than 25 per cent of the total 167.[27] Table 2 shows the numbers of occupations represented by the visually handicapped in six European countries, as well as the numbers of trainees and persons actually working in the occupations, and the percentage of these trainees and workers who needed at least a basic knowledge of Braille in order to be accepted into their particular occupation.

From Table 2 it can be seen that, with the exception of France, slightly over half the jobs occupied by the visually handicapped persons required some knowledge of Braille; approximately two-thirds of trainees and one-half (with the exceptions of Denmark and Sweden) of those actually working are employed in these occupations. These figures would suggest that knowledge of Braille is an important factor in the employment of visually handicapped people, and an increasing trend.

Although about half of the visually handicapped are employed in manual occupations, there is hope that employment opportunities will expand in the future. Some evidence[28] suggests that the range of occupations a visually handicapped person has to choose from is not primarily governed by the limits his handicap places on his capacity, but by traditions and role expectations for the visually handicapped in the particular country he or she is living in. If such diversification of employment is realized, it is likely that it will involve fewer visually handicapped people being employed in traditional craft trades, and more being employed in occupations requiring at least a certain degree of literacy.

A large proportion of the material required by this sector will be for such things as instruction manuals, directories, information leaflets, and other material which shares the characteristic of needing to be updated at fairly regular intervals. This characteristic, together with the need of an increasing number of employed persons to keep or at least have easy access to (sometimes very large) stores of data and information, suggests that some kind of interactive computer system may well provide an essential back-up to many visually handicapped employees. (See Chapter 3.)

Table 2.   Occupations represented by visually handicapped people

Country	Number of occupations	Number of occupations for which Braille required	Number of trainees	Percentage who needed Braille	Number of persons working	Percentage who needed Braille
Denmark	16	10	49	61	146	11
Finland	38	18	101	73	1 919	61
France [1]	6	6	1 164	100	3 439	100
Federal Republic of Germany	26	10	838 [2]	–	9 552	52
Sweden	32	21	70	69	650	31
United Kingdom	38	19	152	76	10 655	47

1. These figures do not include any of the traditional blind trades such as the various craftwork occupations.
2. No details about trainees were given by the Federal Republic of Germany. This figure is taken from a summary table.
Source: Summarized from data in *Training and Employment Opportunities for the Visually Handicapped: A Survey.* WCWB/AMS in collaboration with ILO, Stockholm, 1973.

Casual readers

This is rather a broad category as it involves to some extent all Braille readers, not just those who *only* read for their own entertainment or enlightenment. The material in this section, therefore, can be usefully sub-divided into three: full-length books; magazines, periodicals, etc., not of lasting value; and short material.

Full-length books

Of all the types of Braille materials produced, production of books—from classics to thrillers—is probably the best catered for—although only a small fraction of the print output is available. The development of talking books has had a considerable influence in decreasing demand in some countries for this type of reading material in Braille. However, some people prefer the active reading involved with Braille, rather than the passive, ready-interpreted, listening with talking books.

In support of this there is evidence[29] that in a number of countries—Austria, Belgium, Finland, Hungary, Norway, Spain, Sweden and Yugoslavia—Braille readership is increasing; in Sweden, something like a 25 per cent increase has occurred over the last ten years, after a considerable drop after the introduction of recorded material.

There are other influences causing this increase in Braille readership, however, e.g. increased number of rehabilitation courses for those who have recently become blind, intensified publicity given to Braille, and more effective teaching methods. However, some countries report a reduction of the number of Braille readers of up to as much as 25 per cent, for example, Bulgaria, Czechoslovakia, the Federal Republic of Germany, Italy, Poland and the USSR.[30]

Magazines, periodicals, etc.

This kind of literature has the largest readership with such publications as the radio and television programme guides which cater for virtually all the visually handicapped people who can read Braille. The main characteristic of these sorts of publications is that they do not have lasting value (except, of course, those with a more 'academic' purpose). This material is generally produced at regular intervals—weekly, fortnightly, monthly—and, for Braille, they are produced in large numbers: hundreds or thousands rather than in tens as is more typical of book production. It would seem, then, the factor of prime importance here is that such material should be available at the right time and in sufficient quantities, and any slight reduction in quality is more than compensated for by the advantages of such material being available at all.

Short material

This sort of material is taken for granted by the sighted but is frequently unavailable to the visually handicapped. It includes such material as time-tables, circulars, information leaflets, internal memos, labels, etc. In the United Kingdom, a service system to provide this kind of material, developed at the Warwick Research Unit for the Blind, will be taken over by the Royal National Institute for the Blind.[31] This sort of material is that they do not have lasting value (except, of course, those with a more 'academic' purpose). This material is generally produced at regular intervals—weekly, fortnightly, monthly—and, for Braille, they are produced in large numbers: hundreds or

Aged blind

Numerically, visually handicapped people over 65 years of age comprise about two-thirds of the total visually handicapped population in most developed countries. Their demands for reading material, however, do not reflect their numerical size. This can be illustrated by Table 3 which shows statistics from England and Wales for 1965.

It is probably true to say that persons becoming visually handicapped in their later years are unlikely ever to constitute a large group among Braille readers, mainly because the alternatives now becoming available, such as CCTV and a larger range of recorded material, do not require such a long and arduous training period as Braille before they can be used. In countries where these technical aids are not likely to have such a large effect for some years to come, the elderly will form a not very large part of the demand for casual reading matter described above.

Table 3.   Whether a person was a Braille reader (by age).

Whether a person was a Braille reader	Aged 16–64 %	Aged 65–79 %
Never learned Braille	33	76
Learned, but not good enough to read a book	27	13
Learned, and good enough to read a book	40	11

Source: P. G. Gray and J. E. Todd, *Mobility and Reading Habits of the Blind,* Table 10.5(a), London, HMSO, 1968 (Government Social Survey SS386).

Deaf-blind

Multiple handicapped people are forming an increasing proportion of the visually handicapped population (around 20 per cent in Europe and North America). For some of these multiple handicapped people, Braille is an important medium, as for the deaf-blind for example, where the tactile sensory channel is their main (and, often, only) means for information acquisition. Many of these multiple handicapped will not require Braille, either because of too severe mental retardation, or lack of sufficient muscular control to move their hands over the embossed paper. Nevertheless, there will remain some who are totally dependent on Braille, especially among the deaf-blind, and many who, although not able to cope with the usual Braille that is used, especially in countries where contracted Braille is common, are nonetheless capable of being literate to some extent. There is, therefore, a strong case, not only for uncontracted Braille at least being available, but for material which has been specially written in a simplified form for these people.

The main problem for this group, therefore, lies more in the design of the content and layout of the material, rather than in the actual production of the material itself. This aspect will be considered in more detail in Chapter 2.

In addition to the six areas outlined above, another deserves mention, that is the material required by blind parents with sighted children. Written material can provide an important focal point for interaction between parent and children and there is a significant need for books that can be read visually and tactually. This is also discussed in Chapter 2.

As stated at the beginning of this chapter, statistics involving the visually handicapped, and perhaps particularly Braille readers, should be treated with great caution. Definitions are hazy and generally lack any international standardization. The numbers of internal and external factors are also large. What this latter part of the chapter has tried to show, however, is that gross totals of Braille readers is not that useful to know. Probably over 50 per cent of students use Braille, whereas the corresponding figure for the elderly is probably not more than 5 per cent. Thus, to think in terms of 10–15 per cent of the total population as being Braille readers is not very helpful when planning for provision of Braille material. Also, the type of material needed by the different groups of readers can differ widely, and this has important implications for the development of suitable production equipment. For example, many of the books required by students will be complex, and only required in single copies, whereas large-scale techniques will be required to increase the provision of magazine-type material.

Finally, it is perhaps appropriate to mention one further factor which may have considerable impact on Braille use in the coming years. This is the development of Braille recorders.

The potential impact of Braille recorders

During the mid- to late-1970s, considerable technological development took place in equipment incorporating electromechanical Braille displays. These allow Braille characters to be displayed via a matrix of six metal pins arranged in the standard Braille configuration. Any combination of these six pins can be raised so that any Braille character can become available for tactile reading. Displays, i.e. lines of between twelve and forty-eight such characters, have been constructed and built into equipment which may have considerable impact on the use of Braille. Details of these machines are given in Appendix E.

Just how large this impact will be is, however, rather difficult to predict as there are a number of aspects about which little is known. The most important of these questions is the interaction between machine and user. Nothing is currently known about the readability of metal displays, fatigue during long reading sessions, effect of having only one line available, etc.

The most promising area of use for this equipment is, perhaps, for material required for study or work purposes. For many Braille users their only requirement for Braille is for this type of material and often it is not possible to transcribe this material into Braille as it would be both too bulky and too expensive. This in turn implies that these readers, who are often only mediocre Braille readers anyway, have little opportunity to improve.

With the development of Braille recorders such material becomes cheaper to produce (as no Braille embossing is required) and easier to distribute (one cassette can contain up to about three or four volumes of Braille text). Cassettes can be corrected, up-dated, or otherwise edited, and can be revised many times, which, from the producer's point of view at least, should mean that this form of distribution of Braille material will be of great interest. From the reader's point of view, storage becomes much less of a problem than with conventional Braille books. Also the search facilities available with certain machines mean that any part of the material can be found quickly and easily, thus making them very practical working or studying aids.

Clearly, if Braille printing houses react positively towards this form of Braille distribution, considerable impetus could be given to the use of Braille in the contexts of work and study.

Notes

1. In the richer Western countries, the number of blind is less than 50 per 100,000 inhabitants (0.05 per cent). In poorer countries, there can be over 5,000 per 100,000 inhabitants (5 per cent).
2. H. Pielasch, 'Some Results of the Survey of the European Regional Committee (ERC) about the Activities of Braille Printing Shops and Libraries', *Review of the European Blind* (European Regional Committee of the World Council for the Welfare of the Blind, Paris), No. 1, 1974, p. 10–21.
3. The snellen test is used for testing central visual acuity. A reading of 6/6 means that the individual has normal' vision—that he can read at 6 metres what he ought to be able to read at 6 metres. There are various ratings on a Snellen test, the lowest visual acuity usually being 3/60, which means that the individual can only read at 3 metres what he should be able to read at 60. In the United States feet are read rather than metres so 6/6 is equivalent to 20/20, 6/60 to 20/200 and so on.
4. For example, the classification used by P. G. Gray and J. E. Todd in *Mobility and Reading Habits of the Blind*, London, HMSO, 1968 (Government Social Survey SS386), for determining residual sight useful for reading print was: cannot see windows; can see windows but no more; can see more but did not read large print text; read large print text: (i) but does not generally read ordinary print; (ii) and does generally read ordinary print.
5. Gray and Todd, op. cit.
6. Ibid., p. 76.
7. D. E. Schauder and M. D. Cram, *Libraries for the Blind—An International Study*, Hitchin, Herts, Peter Peregrinus, 1977.
8. M. J. Tobin, *Programmed Instruction and Braille Learning: An Experimental and Multi-Variate Investigation of Some Teaching and Psychological Variables*, p. 2, Birmingham, University of Birmingham School of Education, 1971.
9. *The Education of the Visually Handicapped*, London, HMSO, 1972 (widely known as the 'Vernon Report').
10. J. W. Jones, *Blind Children: Degree of Vision; Mode of Reading*, Washington D.C., US Government Printing Office, 1961 (OE-35026, Bulletin 1961, No. 24).
11. C. Y. Nolan, 'Blind Children: Degree of Vision. A 1963 Replication', *New Outlook for the Blind*, Vol. 59, No. 7, September 1965, p. 233-8.
12. This policy has now changed. See, for example, S. Fine, *Blind and Partially Sighted Children*, p. 20, London, HMSO, 1960.
13. K. Kullberg and J. I. Lindström, *Rehabilitation of the Visually Impaired in the Soviet Union; Report from a Study Tour to Moscow in 1977*, Bromma (Sweden) (Handikappinstitutet Gröna Serien 7/77).
14. Vernon Report, op. cit.
15. P. A. Kolers, 'Sensory Supplementation: Reading', in: M. Graham (ed.), *Science and Blindness: Retrospective and Prospective*, p. 145, New York, N.Y., American Foundation for the Blind, 1972.
16. For example, from RCEVH, University of Birmingham (see Appendix D 4).
17. M. D. Graham, 'Towards a Functional Definition of Blindness', *New Outlook for the Blind*, Vol. 53, 1959, p. 285-8.
18. Using a definition of 20/200 a survey of the American blind population arrived at a population of approximately 400,000. A survey using a functional definition—not being able to read newsprint, even with the aid of lenses—arrived at a figure of approximately 1 million. See also, R. J. Hurlin, *Estimated Prevalence of Blindness in the US*, New York, N.Y., American Foundation for the Blind, 1953.
19. The doctrine of 'saving sight' is followed in the Soviet Union. (See Kullberg and Lindström, op. cit.).
20. A. Shaw, *Print for Partial Sight*, London, Library Association, 1969.

21. D. Dallas, *Survey of Study Techniques and Media Used by the Visually Handicapped Students*, ABAPSTAS, 1974. (Available from T. Moody, Department of Political Economy, University of Glasgow, Scotland.)

22. Cf. discussion of residual vision and mode of reading above.

23. P. W. Nye and J. C. Bliss, 'Sensory Aids for the Blind: A Challenging Problem with Lessons for the Future', *IEEE Proceedings*, Vol. 58, No. 12, December 1970.

24. S. Genensky, 'A Functional Classification of the Visually Impaired to Replace the Legal Definition of Blindness', *Teacher of the Blind*, Vol. LXI, No. 3, April 1973, p. 83–90.

25. L. H. Goldish, *Braille in the United States: Its Production, Distribution and Use*, New York, N.Y., American Foundation for the Blind, 1967.

26. A. Sorsby, *The Incidence and Causes of Blindness in England and Wales, 1963–1968*, p. 31, London, HMSO, 1972 (Report on Public Health and Medical Subjects, 28).

27. M. Myrberg, 'Role and Importance of the Statistics of the WCWB International Investigation of Training and Employment Opportunities for the Visually Handicapped in Vocational Rehabilitation of the Blind', in B. Lindquist (ed.), *Report on European Seminar Concerning 'The Training and Employment Situation of the Blind'*, p. 3–14, Brussels, 1973.

28. Myrberg, op. cit.

29. Pielasch, op. cit.

30. Ibid.

31. J. M. Gill and J. B. Humphreys, 'A Feasibility Study on a Braille Transcription Service for Short Documents', *Braille Automation Newsletter* (Warwick Research Unit for the Blind), August 1976, p. 19-24.

32. B. E. Hampshire, *Production av punktskrift i mindre skala* [Report], Bromma (Sweden), Handikapp-institutet, 1980 (Order No. X201). (In Swedish only.)

Chapter 2

Selection, editing and distribution of Braille material

Introduction

This chapter is concerned with what Goldish has called the 'Braille System' which he describes as follows:

[The model of Braille production and distribution] can be segmented into three elements—input, production, and distribution—each of which performs a distinct activity. The system is activated by a fourth element, the Braille readers, and it functions amidst a environment of social, political and economic factors.[1]

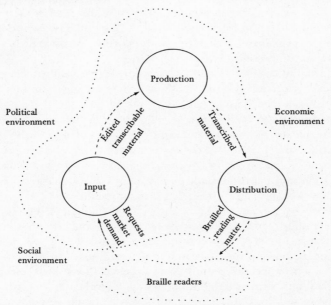

Fig. 1.   Model of the Braille production and distribution system.

The input element transforms a reader's request or market demand into a form suitable for transcription into Braille. The production element transforms inkprint into Braille. The distribution element disseminates the brailled material from the producer to the Braille reader. It is important to remember, however, as Goldish states, 'each of these elements ... is ... a skilled person or, in the case of distribution, an individual or organization. Any devices used are incidental to the process. The human is the major functioning component.'[2]

In this chapter 'input' and 'distribution' are discussed in some detail. 'Input' involves ways in which material is selected for transcribing and why and how this material is edited so that it is appropriate for the medium of Braille. 'Distribution' is concerned simply with the different ways of organizing delivery of the Braille to the reader. The two remaining elements included in Goldish's model—'production' and 'Braille readers'—are discussed in detail in Chapters 3 and 1 respectively.

Input

Selection of material for transcribing

The resources available for Braille publishing are such that only a small proportion of the literature available to sighted readers can be available to Braille readers. The decisive factor responsible for this situation is the small number of Braille readers, thereby only permitting small production runs, rather than any inherent and costly factor in the actual production process. Aspects relating to Braille readership were discussed in Chapter 1 and it was argued there that Braille readership is not likely to increase significantly in the foreseeable future. This implies that the high cost of Braille is likely to remain, even though some reduction in cost may be achieved by rationalization in the production process.

This, in turn, implies that an effective organization to deal with requests and to satisfy the market demand for Braille material is an essential requirement of a Braille publishing house and/or library.

The first decision to be made regarding the selection of material concerns allocating available resources between the different areas of need, such as material for school children, students, magazine material, novels, etc. In some cases, the production facilities may be part of a general organization of or for the blind, in which case certain areas may gain automatic priority or, on the other hand, be eliminated, according to the constitution of the general organization.

Once the level of production for each area has been budgeted for, there are two ways in which Braille readers influence the selection of books or other material to be transcribed. First, by directly requesting specific titles and, secondly, through borrowing and/or buying trends creating a general 'readers profile'. The printing house editor and his selection committee try to reflect this in their selection, among other considerations, such as general popularity, topicality, significance, etc.

Before discussing these two aspects, however, it should be pointed out that all Braille material is not a more or less direct translation of existing inkprint material.

Many organizations of and for the visually handicapped produce their own magazines containing information and news just of relevance to certain special interest groups among the visually handicapped. Also, some printing houses produce weekly summaries of news and events of general topical interest. However, the visually handicapped as a group in society have additional, specialized information needs, relating to certain social, educational, environmental and political questions which have, or ought to have, special significance for the visually handicapped, e.g. changes in school curricula, changes in public transport or traffic systems, special aids and concessions. Often such changes are carried out with just the general population in mind; these changes must be made known to the visually handicapped population and they must be given an opportunity to comment where the changes do not benefit them as much as they do the sighted population. This kind of specialized material, written and/or selected with the visually handicapped in mind, is an important function of any information/editorial department associated with a Braille printing house.

Requests

This type of direct selection from the readers is usually for special groups or needs such as school children (via their teachers), students, and employed visually handicapped who require material for their work.

This type of production reflects the 'service' function of many Braille printing houses. That is to say, they fulfil an essential need on an individual level, in a way which few ordinary printing houses do.

The amount of such individual material any printing house carries out depends on the external economical, social and political influences included in Goldish's model, e.g. whether financial help for individuals wanting material transcribed is available or the extent to which there are private and/or volunteer transcribing services available.

In countries which have considerable de-centralized production facilities, usually in the form of home-working volunteer transcriber groups, there is an important need for all Braille production to be catalogued. In countries where production is confined to one or two places, this creates less of a problem, although it is of course just as necessary to have such a catalogue. Braille is time- and money-consuming to produce and it is vital that the first step be to check whether a book is already available in Braille before embarking on a transcription.

Most of the major printing houses have such catalogues, as do Braille libraries. In the United States, the *General Catalog of Volunteer-Produced Textbooks* is kept at the American Printing House and the *Union Catalog of Hand-Copied Books* at the Library of Congress. Towards the end of 1978, the Organización Nacional de Ciegos under the direction of Pedro Zurita, was preparing a list of printing houses and libraries for the blind, and periodicals, covering such relevant information as the availability of Braille music, etc.[3]

Market demand

The selection of inkprint books other than those specifically requested is carried out
with many of the same criteria as books for public libraries.

There has been some debate on the question of to what extent selection of books
in a Braille library should reflect that of an ordinary one. There are some who argue
from the point of view that the reading interests of the visually handicapped do not
differ from those of the sighted and the content of a Braille library should therefore
reflect this. Others, however, maintain that certain types of books are more popular
among Braille readers—a conclusion usually based on the buying/borrowing
statistics of Braille readers—which do not necessarily correspond to those most
popular among the sighted. Some compromise is, therefore, usually sought between
trying to publish a reasonably wide selection of books in Braille, in order to stimulate
interest, and satisfying known readers' interests.

At the Royal National Institute for the Blind (RNIB) in London the selection
process for Braille books is particularly well developed and is worth describing in
some detail. RNIB's policy on Braille publishing is to divide its allocation for this
purpose into two—half for specialist use (mainly schools) and half for general use.

As regards provision of books for schools (i.e. special schools for the blind), there is
a sub-committee of the College of Teachers of the Blind which advises each year on
which books are required by schools. This committee tries to co-ordinate school needs
as far as possible in order to provide RNIB with orders of at least forty.

It is the job of the publishing editor to recommend which books are to be
transcribed with the other half of the allocation, and any other specialist material,
such as a programming manual, an official report, or similar, which is to come out of
the 'specialist' half of the money. His recommendations are based on reviews and
bestseller lists with the intention of trying to reflect the present output of the printing
houses as representatively as possible. However, when the total yearly Braille output is
only about 2.5 per cent of the yearly output of print books in the United Kingdom, this
is a very difficult task, especially as these small numbers cover a wide range of interests
and requirements. The publications editor thus produces a list of books to be
published during the next three months. These are discussed, and the final titles
decided upon by a Publications Committee.

These titles are then advertised in the *New Beacon,* a journal published by RNIB,
together with a short description of their content. The books appear in three
successive issues of the *New Beacon,* and the numbers of orders received during this
period help determine what kind of publication a particular book is to be (if enough
orders are received, that is, for it to be published at all): there are three types. There is
the permanent stock, which are books that are kept in stock all the time at RNIB, so
that these titles are always available. They are automatically reprinted if the numbers
in stock fall below three. The other two types of publication are the limited
editions—one where plates are retained so that if sufficient orders are received for
that book after the first printing has been sold, it can be reprinted. The other type of
limited edition is where the plates are destroyed as soon as that edition has been
printed. This replaces an earlier system which kept all plates, and automatically
replenished falling stocks irrespective of the demand for that book.

One additional factor relevant to publishing and distribution is the size of the language area in which the book is published. Clearly, the potential market for a book published in English or Spanish is vastly greater than one published in Swedish or Dutch, for example. Similarly, there is a much greater quantity of material in the former languages available for transcription. In this context, the possibility for utilizing the widest possible international market for distributing Braille books is important. However, international copyright laws can create problems in some cases. Investigations into this aspect are currently being carried out by Cylke[4] and Nowill.[5]

Editing

Choice of media

In countries having facilities to produce both Braille and talking books, the first decision to be made is the choice of media.

In the case of general reading matter this will largely depend on the existing facilities, money available (talking books are cheaper and quicker to produce than Braille) and general policy. In the case of more complex material for more limited consumption, books requested by students for example, the decision is rather more involved. The discussion in this section will, therefore, be mainly with study, or similar, material in mind, although many aspects will also apply to other, simpler kinds of literature.

Choice of media, then, depends on the reader's proficiency at Braille, the nature of the book and how quickly it is needed. Complex formats in Braille books, and especially the use of relief diagrams, demands a high degree of expertise in Braille and tactile reading on the part of the reader.

The presentation of complex and/or highly interrelated information can often be difficult to do in sequential form, as talking books necessarily are. Textbooks are rarely read from beginning to end: certain chapters are read before others and chapters or smaller chunks of text are read over and over again—these sections may be widely spread within the book; access to certain paragraphs may be needed often and quickly. Such a pattern of usage is suited more to a conventional book format rather than to speech on tape.

Practical considerations may outweigh educational factors; a well-designed Braille book is no use if it only comes in time for the end of the student's course! Talking books take less time to produce than Braille books, and if the book involves complex formats it is unlikely that computer-aided production can be utilized to any great extent to reduce this difference in production times. Even if the book is to be produced as a talking book, this can still allow for certain 'supplements' being produced in Braille or relief diagrams.

Format

Relative to inkprint, Braille is a very inflexible medium, and in many ways any medium developed for the tactile sense must be so. The capabilities of the tactile sense to perceive the layout of text on a page, or a relief diagram, or to jump to and from text to footnote, or text to diagram, are considerably more limited than those of the visual sense. The reader of Braille, and especially Braille of a more complex nature, must rely on 'convention' in order to compensate for the lack of ability to gain a quick, general overview of a page. The Braille reader should be able to feel certain that the page numbers are always located in the same place on the page, and that the legend of diagrams and maps are located in the same place in relation to them. Similarly, that tables of contents, indexes, reference lists, etc., are always laid out in the same way and that diagrams are always labelled in the same way, etc. In short, a Braille book should be edited so as to limit, as far as possible, the need to search and/or cross-associate different parts of the text.

In general, however, it is usually recommended that the format of the original print book be followed as far as possible. Aspects which a Braille editor usually needs to give special attention to are the following: illustrated material, such as figures, diagrams, pictures, etc.; tables; prefaces, forewords, introductions, indices, appendices, glossaries, bibliographies; page numbering; and foreign words.

Illustrative material

Myrberg in his study of graphical information in talking books,[6] found that 'text books in the talking-book libraries indicate that the development towards "visualised" text books has not meant that an increased share of the information in text books is conveyed graphically. There has been an increased use of illustrations in text books, but no substantial increase in the information conveyed by them. At the same time the studies of text books in the talking-book libraries showed that there were figures that conveyed very much and very important information.'

The selection of figures for reproduction in relief form or for written description in the text is a fairly involved question. A separate section will, therefore, be devoted to this together with discussion of the available methods for producing relief material.

Tables

These can be included in the text or, if of a particularly complex type or if referred to in the text often, it can be written as a separate appendix.

Tables in print often function in books as a way of summarizing information or presenting a large amount of information only a part of which is perhaps essential for the reader to know. Thus, the editor must decide in the former case whether such summarizing of information which has already been presented in the text serves any essential function. In the latter case a table's contents may be reduced so that only that which is essential is included. This may involve discussion with the author or, more usually, a specialist in the subject of the book.

Print allows, through the use of different sizes of type fonts and line spacing, considerable flexibility regarding fitting and adapting the contents of a table into a visually clear pattern. Such flexibility is not available in Braille. This means that a

Braille table may have to be set out such that the text usually written as a column on the left of the table in print is written out across the whole line, or even take two or more lines. The columns of values are then written, spaced as in columns on the next line. Thus the 'table' consists of alternate lines of text and values. (See Plate 3.)

Or, for large tables with many columns of values, the usual table format can be dispensed with completely. Instead the table headings are given first, with appropriate abbreviations, as a separate paragraph of text. Then each row of values is given as a separate paragraph. Each paragraph is headed with what the row of values refers to and each value is preceded by its column's abbreviation.

Prefaces, forewords, etc.

These should generally be included and should conform as far as possible to the original print with regard to content and to a Braille convention with regard to layout. For example, each beginning a new page, headings centred on the third line and separated by a single blank line from the first line of text.[7]

Page numbers referred to in indices should, naturally, be the Braille page numbers and not the original print page references.

Page numbers

Again a certain convention should be followed. For example, only the page to the right of the binding is numbered, with the number written at the end of the uppermost line of the page, or every page is numbered with the number centred on the uppermost line.

One convention used by American authorities which is both practical and realistic is as follows:

If, in checking the page numbering, it is discovered that a page number has been repeated, the repetition sign, dots 5 & 6, should be placed immediately before the number sign on the page on which the duplication has been made. If it is discovered that a page number has been omitted, the omission sign, dot 5, should be placed immediately before the number sign on the page on which the omission has been made.[8]

Foreign words

Each system of contracted Braille will usually have its own conventions regarding whether contractions may be used in foreign words. Most, however, prohibit or limit the use of contractions in such contexts.

One source of difficulty with regard to foreign codes is that, despite the fact the basic alphabetical letters of European languages are standardized, accented letters are not. Table 1 illustrates this point.

The Braille editor must, therefore, decide when to write a foreign word or words in the Braille code of the foreign language or the Braille code of the country where the book is being written and is to be read. Some convention should ideally exist for these occurrences so that the reader is always clear as to which Braille code the foreign word is written in.

Table 1.
Table illustrating different Braille codes for accented vowels

	á	à	é	è	í	ì	ó	ò	ú	ù
Czech	•	–	•	–	–	–	•	–	•	–
Dutch (for foreign words)	–	•	•	•	–	•	–	•	–	•
French	–	•	•	•	–	–	–	–	–	•
Gaelic	•	–	•	–	•	–	•	–	–	•
Hungarian	•	–	•	–	•	–	•	–	•	–
Icelandic	•	–	•	–	•	–	•	–	•	–
Italian	–	–	–	–	•	–	–	–	–	•
Portuguese	•	•	•	•	–	•	–	•	•	•
Polish	–	–	–	–	–	–	•	–	•	–
Spanish	•	–	•	–	•	–	•	–	•	–

Illustrative material in Braille books

As mentioned above, the use of illustrations in books, and especially textbooks, has increased considerably during recent years. Yet Myrberg has found that often these illustrations are not essential in order for the book to be understood by the reader.[9] For the editor of a Braille book, then, the evaluation of the 'information content' or 'usefulness' of an illustration is an important process as conversion of illustrative material to a form which makes it available to a visually handicapped reader is a difficult and involved process.

Types of figures

Myrberg has analysed textbook illustrations using a classification scheme developed by Ackoff;[10] there are three different types: (a) illustrations showing what something looks like he calls *Iconic* figures, e.g. are pictures or drawings of objects; (b) illustrations showing an aspect or dimension of a certain phenomenon, such as the number of voters for different political parties, he calls *Analogue* figures, e.g. diagrams and maps with legends; (c) illustrations showing a phenomenon's or object's relations to another phenomenon or object he calls *Symbolic* figures, e.g. organization charts, flow charts, etc.

Iconic figures are the least complicated, then come analogue and the most complicated are symbolic figures. In other words, the information content increases from iconic, through analogue, to symbolic figures.

Assigning figures in a text to one of these categories is not always easy, but it is important, as the amount of information lost by leaving out a figure that is information-rich and the amount of time and money wasted producing a superfluous illustration in relief form are significant. Often good clues can be found in the text. If, for example, it is stated 'in Fig. 10 is shown an example of . . .' this usually refers to an iconic figure. If it is stated 'in Fig. 11 one can see the different amounts of . . .', this refers to an analogue figure. If it is stated 'Fig. 12 shows the structure of . . .', this refers to a symbolic figure.

The loss of information caused by leaving out an iconic figure is often marginal compared to analogue or symbolic figures; therefore, it is more important to be able to distinguish iconic figures from the other two than it is to distinguish between analogue and symbolic figures.

Deciding on what to do with figures

As a general principle, iconic figures can be left out, assuming that the figure does not contain information needed in exercises, etc. Analogue and symbolic figures should, however, be included in some form. These figures can, however, give rise to another problem—the editor doesn't know the subject well enough to be able to understand what the author wants to say with a figure. One possibility is to contact an expert in the subject concerned and obtain either a written description of the information contained in the figure or advice on how it might be simplified for reproduction in relief form.

Myrberg says the following about relief diagrams:

The production of raised-line material is rather time consuming. Moreover, there are no commonly accepted conventions concerning symbols in relief graphs. It is also dangerous to overestimate the potentials of relief representation. The tactile reading of a raised-line graph is much more difficult than the visual reading of an 'inkprint' graph. The initial overview that is acquired rather easily when the figure is inspected visually is a rather complicated matter when it comes to tactile reading. Isolated parts of the figure are sequentially and gradually built up into a whole when the figure is read tactually. There is a saying that reading a raised-line map tactually is like reading a wall map visually with a magnifying glass. A raised-line figure can thus not be considered a simple equivalent alternative to the inkprint figure . . . the difficulties and drawbacks with relief presentation of figures must not be interpreted as advice to refrain from this form of representation.[11]

Practical and economic considerations also play a significant part in this decision. If only one person needs the book, and fairly urgently, some quicker and cheaper alternative should be found, e.g. a written description, or, if it is a student who requires the book, his/her teacher or tutor could be contacted in order to explain the figure.

Careful consideration of the following aspects should be made, therefore, before embarking on a relief representation of a figure. Can the figure be left out completely? Can the information conveyed by the diagram be described in the text instead? Does the person receiving the book have someone (e.g. teacher) who can explain and describe the figure? Is it possible to convert the diagram to a relief form which is readable? Are time, personnel and resources available to produce a relief figure?

With regard to principles of design for relief figures, no real standards or conventions exist. In general, the most important aspect to control is the density of information in the tactile figure; visual figures usually are far too complex and 'dense' to be simply converted to a relief form. Extensive editing of the figure is normally required, and this will often require consultation with a subject specialist to decide which parts may be simplified or deleted.

Myrberg presented a decision tree for the choice of form of reproduction of graphical material in talking books which has been slightly modified to be more relevant to Braille book production. (Fig. 2.)

This decision tree should not be followed slavishly, of course. The person ordering the book may ask for a certain form of representation and this should, whenever possible, be given. In situations where the editor is a little uncertain, however, this tree may help to suggest the most appropriate direction to take.

Production of tactile graphic material

There are many different ways of producing tactile graphic material and these have been reviewed in the literature.[12] A short description of the six most usual or appropriate for illustrative material for books is given below (see also Appendix B 5).

Spur wheel. This is simply a wheel with points around its circumference. This wheel can be moved over the reverse side of the paper thereby causing a punctate line to be embossed on the other side. By using different shapes of spur on the wheel a variety of punctate lines can be produced, but, nevertheless, the technique is limited to rather simple linear diagrams.

Upward relief drawers. There are many kits available for drawing directly on to special plastic sheets. The action of the 'pen' on the plastic is such that an upward raised line is produced in the plastic following the pen's movement. This technique has similar limitations to the spur wheel.

Figure drawers. A number of similar machines has been developed based on the idea of a stylus moving over a writing table according to the outline of the figure to be produced in relief. This stylus can be moved freely in any direction by hand. Under the stylus and connected to it via an arm is an embossing pin which moves such that it is always directly under the stylus. During movement the pin embosses a punctate line. There exist machines similar in concept which can emboss metal plates, aluminum foil, plastic and paper.

Master allowing vacuum-form copying. This method is probably the one in most widespread use. It involves the building up of a master on a paper base using cardboard, wire, sandpaper, etc., which can then be vacuum-formed. The materials making up the master are chosen to give shapes and textures in the vacuum-formed plastic. There are many variations of this basic approach.

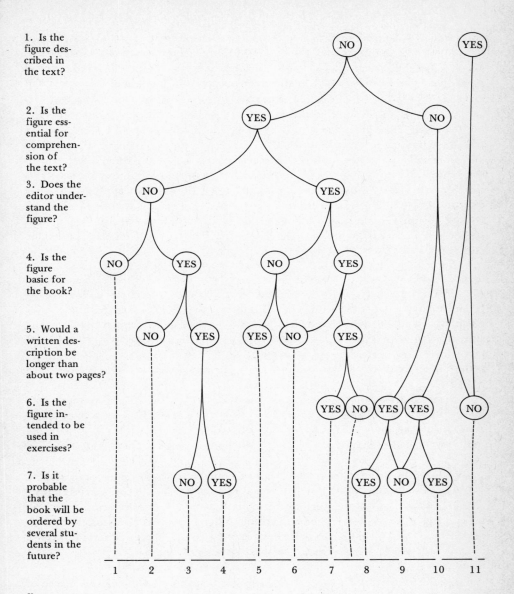

1. Is the figure described in the text?

2. Is the figure essential for comprehension of the text?

3. Does the editor understand the figure?

4. Is the figure basic for the book?

5. Would a written description be longer than about two pages?

6. Is the figure intended to be used in exercises?

7. Is it probable that the book will be ordered by several students in the future?

Key:
1 = Reference to teacher or tutor or similar person; 2 = Description should be made by a subject matter expert; 3 = Reference to teacher or tutor or similar person; 4 = Relief figure and reference to teacher or similar; 5 = Reference to teacher or tutor or similar person; 6 = Editor's description; 7 = Relief figure and reference to teacher or similar person; 8 = Relief figure, supplemented by editor's description; 9 = Reference to teacher or tutor or similar person; 10 = Relief figure; 11 = The figure is excluded.

Fig. 2. Decision tree for the choice of form of representation of graphical material in Braille books.

Photo-etching.   A more sophisticated technique is photo-etching a plate consisting of light-sensitive plastic permanently laminated to a metal base by means of an adhesive layer. When the plate is exposed to ultra-violet light, the plastic polymerizes, i.e. all parts that have been exposed to the light become hardened and insoluble. The unexposed parts of the plate can be removed with solvent. Thus, any pattern can be created in relief on the plate by covering it with a photographic transparency, thereby only exposing those parts that are required to be in relief to the ultra-violet light. As both a positive and negative of the transparency can be obtained, corresponding male and female plates can be produced. This technique is used in the Federal Republic of Germany to produce relief material, although they only produce a single plate and this is then used as a master for vacuum-forming plastic. This approach has the disadvantage of it being necessary to bore small air holes in the plate before vacuum-forming as the plate is not porous to air. The technique has been used successfully in Sweden, with two plates pressing out the relief drawing on Braille paper in a hand-fed flat-bed press.

Screen printing.   An approach has been investigated in the Federal Republic of Germany using a special foam-forming paste which swells when heated. This ink can be applied to the paper by the normal silk-screen process. The screen mask can either be produced manually or by a photographic process. Once printed, the material should be cured for one or two minutes at about 180 °C immediately after the printing procedure. This causes the ink to swell up and they become available to touch. Different elevations can be achieved by overprinting and different colours are available.

There is no shortage of ideas and (technically) possible alternative approaches to the production of tactile graphic material. However, relatively few of the available methods are in any regular use. Any new production method must deal with the following problems involved with the production of tactile graphic material.

Time.   Most current techniques are labour intensive and take a long time to carry out. Any new technique must reduce this production time.

Editing and design.   Design of a tactile figure is an involved process and at present there is no collective agreement concerning design principles and symbol standardization. Any new technique must be flexible and easy to change and modify so as to obtain the best possible design in the shortest possible time.

Cost.   Currently this is a large prohibitive factor to the more widespread use of tactile material. Most production at present is so labour intensive its real cost is very high. The fact that a new technique is as cheap as possible is therefore an important factor.

These problems in producing good tactile figures are in part responsible for the relatively few people who can use them *effectively*. Tactile reading of spatial patterns is a difficult process and something which should be learnt when young if possible. Production of raised material for school children who are severely visually impaired should therefore be an area to concentrate on in regard to provision of such material.

Combined visual and tactile presentation

Books provide a common form of interaction between a child and his parents or his peers. If the child or the parent(s) is/are blind, this form of interaction is considerably hampered. Some trials have been made in order to try and produce books that can be available both visually and tactually. This has been carried out most successfully by the Howe Press (Appendix B 1). They took a typical children's book and unbound it. The pages were then embossed with Braille text corresponding to the written text on the pages. Usually the amount of text on a page of a children's book is small so that there is room for the Braille on the same page. In cases where this is not possible, however, a clear plastic sheet is embossed and inserted between the pages.

Such a technique allows a blind parent, for example, to read a story together with his/her sighted child or vice-versa. Obviously the numerous pictures common in children's books cannot be transferred to a tactile form also, but, nevertheless, such modification can mean a great deal to promoting interaction between sighted and blind and, in the case of blind children, promoting early tactile and reading practice.

Distribution

Most of the Braille books that are produced by central or regional printing facilities are distributed via a Braille library. The organization of this distribution as well as its extent varies considerably. Some basic details of a number of Braille libraries, including the size and type of their stock and whether they loan books abroad, are given in Appendix A.

Loans from a central library

It is not unusual in current Braille production systems that the majority of general Braille books are produced in only one copy. In many countries, these are produced by homeworkers, either paid or volunteer, and thus some centralized facility to distribute this production is required.

Such a centralized facility must keep a record of the various books being transcribed at any one time and keep the catalogues up to date. Actual distribution is carried out by post in most cases in response to a request. Such distribution of Braille books is appropriate for Braille in the majority of countries owing to the difficulty and expense of Braille production and the relatively few readers among the visually handicapped population.

De-centralized lending

Ideally, a Braille reader should be able to go to his/her local library to obtain Braille books. Considerable steps towards such de-centralized distribution have been for large print and talking books. Such distribution for Braille books is more unlikely, however, while numbers of Braille readers remain so few.

Some limited de-centralized distribution is possible, however, where there is no central organization to administer centralized lending system. This involves the automatic distribution of all production from a printing house to certain organizations of and for the blind, some larger print libraries, special schools, etc. Such distribution is often inefficient, however, due to the lack of contact between producers and consumers.

Selling Braille books

A number of countries produce Braille books which are sold. Their selling price does not reflect their cost of production so considerable financial support is necessary before such distribution is possible. A common way of setting the price of the Braille books is to charge the same as the original print book. For this type of production to be effective, close contact must be possible between the readers and producers so that production can be closely geared to readers' needs.

Computer-assisted book-lending systems

Many libraries for the visually handicapped have experienced considerable increases in the number of loans they are having to deal with. This increase has been the result of introducing talking books which are far more accessible to the majority of the visually handicapped, especially the elderly, than Braille books.

Such increases in readership have stimulated a number of countries, e.g. the Netherlands, to consider computerizing their book lending system. At the Dutch Library for the Blind, their computer will hold the complete catalogue, it will do all lending administration and it will log the books sent out and returned. Van Vliet has written a fairly detailed description of this system.[13]

Impact of recent technological developments

Current technological developments, especially in the field of telecommunications, will almost certainly have considerable implications for the distribution of books and information in Braille.

The crucial development has been of equipment incorporating a Braille display (see Appendix E). Information encoded either in a computer or on some machine-readable medium, such as paper-tape (the latter is possible without having a computer as such, see for example System IV, Chapter 3), can be 'distributed' electronically, over the telephone network, for example, to such Braille display equipment. The costs of such electronic equipment are decreasing every year so that utilization of such equipment by individuals, as opposed to organizations or companies, is realistic.

At present, too little is known about the human factors involved with the use of such mechanical Braille displays. If they find acceptance among Braille readers, however, their use could provide very significant motivation for many more people to learn Braille and, perhaps as a secondary consequence, increase the demand for ordinary Braille book production.

Notes

1. L. H. Goldish, *Braille in the US: Its Production, Distribution and Use*, p. 53, New York, N.Y., American Foundation for the Blind (AFB), 1967.
2. Ibid.
3. Personal communication, 29 November 1978, from Pedro Zurita, Head of International Relations Department, Organización Nacional de Ciegos, Madrid (Spain).
4. Frank Kurt Cylke, Library of Congress, 1291 Taylor Street NW, Washington, D.C. (United States).
5. Ms Dorina de Gouvea Nowill, Committee on Cultural Affairs, World Council for the Welfare of the Blind (WCWB), Rua Dr Diego de Faria 558, 04037 São Paulo (Brazil).
6. M. Myrberg, *Towards an Ergonomic Theory of Text Design and Composition*, Stockholm, Almqvist & Wiksell, 1978 (Uppsala Studies in Education, 5).
7. M. B. Dorf and E. R. Scharry, *Instruction Manual for Braille Transcribing*, Washington, D.C., Library of Congress, Division of the Blind, 1961.
8. Ibid.
9. Myrberg, op. cit.
10. R. Ackoff, *Scientific Method: Optimizing Applied Research Decisions*, New York, N.Y., John Wiley, 1962.
11. Myrberg, op. cit., p. 82.
12. See for example, J. M. Gill, 'Tactile Mapping', *AFB Research Bulletin*, No. 28, October 1974, p. 57–80 (includes a comprehensive bibliography); A. M. Kidwell and P. S. Greer, *Sites, Perception and the Non-Visual Experience; AFB State of the Art Report*, New York, N.Y., American Foundation for the Blind, 1973; B. E. Hampshire, 'The Design and Production of Tactile Graphic Material for the Visually Impaired', *Applied Ergonomics*, Vol. 10, No. 2, June 1979, p. 87–92.
13. R. Van Vliet, 'Computer Assisted Book-Lending System for the Blind', *Braille Research Newsletter*, No. 8, September 1978, p. 88–104.

Chapter 3

The production
of Braille

Introduction

Development of techniques for Braille production was considerable during the 1960s and 1970s. These developments, however, were largely concentrated in just a few countries and to a large extent involved the utilization of sophisticated techniques.

These new techniques have introduced a great variety in the type of production systems possible. There are now choices of equipment for each stage of the production process. These are discussed separately under five headings, corresponding to the main stages of the production process, namely: input forms, proof reading and correction, computer-aided translation of print to Braille, Braille embossing equipment, and post-embossing operations.

It is of the greatest importance to transfer these new techniques to as many countries as possible, yet, at the same time, this must not take place in a simple 'transfer of technology' sense. The new production methods introduced must be appropriate to the conditions existing in the printing house and the country in general. Thus, some discussion is given to factors relevant to the design of Braille production and these are illustrated by five examples.

In the final section two areas requiring more specialized Braille production equipment are discussed. These are concerned with Braille as a working communication medium rather than just a reading medium. The potential for developing the use of Braille in the future will, to a large extent, depend on the ability of people to use it efficiently in a work and study environment. It is, furthermore, just this aspect which has most to benefit from current developments in electronics and telecommunications and their application to Braille equipment.

Writing Braille

A major factor in the emergence of Braille as the medium of communication favoured by the visually handicapped was that it could both be written and read. Various other forms of raised types which were competing with Braille at the end of the last century were, by and large, only reading mediums.

The first Braille books—the Bible in most countries—were produced by hammering out every individual dot in sheets of metal with a hammer and stylus. These plates could then be used to emboss paper on an ordinary printing press. This form of writing on paper is still in common use today in the form of the 'Slate and Stylus'.

For many thousands of Braille users, this form of writing Braille is their equivalent of a note- or writing pad. Each dot is pressed out downwards using the 'windows' in the slate as a template. As the Braille cells have to be written downwards they must also be written back-to-front so that they will be correct when the paper is turned over.

An important factor in the emergence of Braille as the superior communication medium for the visually handicapped was the development of mechanical Braillewriters. These mainly consisted of six keys, one corresponding to each of the dots in the Braille cell, and a spacing key. The operation of these keys caused dots to be embossed in paper by blunt styli connected to the keys.

There are a considerable number of Braillewriters now available (see Appendix B for details). There are two fundamental characteristics by which Braillewriters should be distinguished. The first is whether they are downward or upward writing. 'Downward' writers, e.g. the British Stainsby machine, have the major disadvantage of not allowing immediate inspection of what has been written. Although there are a number of such machines still in use, most modern Braillewriters are 'upward' writers. This means that the cells are embossed from underneath the paper which means that they can be seen or felt directly after embossing.

The second characteristic is whether the Braillewriter can write on both sides of the paper or on only one side. The modern upward Braillewriters—e.g. the Perkins machine or the Marburg Braillewriter—are not constructed to write on both sides of the paper. It is probably this factor which keeps old machines such as the Stainsby in use; its ability to write interpoint or interline Braille is just about its only positive characteristic.[1]

The Braillewriter most widely used today is the American Perkins machine manufactured by the Howe Press of the Perkins School for the Blind. More than 115,000 Perkins have now been sold and continue to be sold at a rate of approximately 9,000 a year.[2] Despite the popularity of the Perkins, however, a constantly recurring request from many Braille users is for a portable, silent and cheap Braillewriters which preferably can write on both sides of the paper. Furthermore, it should be ideally be electrically driven to reduce the stress to the finger and forearm muscles.

This need may, in part, be met by the mechanical braille display equipment now becoming available (see Appendix E).

Braille duplicating equipment

The equipment described here can be regarded as miniature production systems, although they can be used for medium as well as small runs, i.e. up to about 100 copies. Their main disadvantage is that they are slow and can be tedious to operate. However, in situations where time is not a dominating factor and labour is relatively cheap, they can offer a very practical solution to the problem of Braille production.

Marburg Braille duplicator (see Appendix B 2)

This duplicator is designed for the reproduction of Braille texts in small and medium quantities.

The system consists of a type frame in which five type blocks can be mounted. The Braille characters are composed from three type segments which either contain two dots, one dot or no dots. In this way a Braille page consisting of twenty-five lines of twenty-eight characters each can be set. Paper is then placed over these type segments and a pressure roller, which is an integral part of the duplicator, is run over the paper causing it to be embossed by the raised type segments.

It is possible to emboss interpoint Braille with this equipment and any number of copies can be printed. The size of the equipment is 610 × 300 × 160 mm and it weighs 17.5 kg.

Hardening of paper to make a press master

This technique has quite a long history and a number of different methods have been tried. The principle involved is to harden the Braille sheet in some way so that it can be used as a master plate for pressing out multiple copies on paper using some kind of press.

A number of different substances have been tried for hardening the embossed paper. In the *Guerin* process, developed in France, the paper is first coated with shellac on the embossed side then the reverse side is coated with a special plaster. The *Uformite* process uses a relatively thin film of urea-formaldehyde resin instead of plaster.

Of techniques available for purchasing the *Espinasse duplicator* (see Appendix B 2) can be mentioned. It functions as follows:

Text is written in Braille by means of ordinary machine on offset paper, then hardened by dipping in silicate bath. Used as master plate in manual press. From well-prepared original, it is possible to make 12–100 copies or more.[3]

Another variation has been developed by Beatty (see Appendix B 2), who describes the technique as follows:

In my process, Thermoform plastic sheets are embossed in the normal manner using a Perkins Brailler or other suitable means. The embossed plastic sheet is then turned upside down and the indentations for each dot filled with a water-based putty.

The back filled sheet may be wrapped on the drum of any of several kinds of duplicating machines and paper to be embossed is rolled between the plastic master and a rubber blanket.

(Either copy paper or Braille manilla can be used.) Braille manilla does not give quite as high or sharp dot. However, by a slight modification of the Perkins Brailler a higher dot can be produced which gives very good Braille on manilla.[4]

The main disadvantage of this technique is that only single-sided Braille can be produced.

The *vacuum-forming* process allows the immediate copying of single-sided Braille or any relief form from a paper master.

The copies are produced by placing the master on the platen of the machine. A sheet of plastic is placed over this master and clamped in place by a frame. The plastic is then heated so that it becomes fairly soft. A vacuum is applied which forces the plastic sheet down over the master such that the plastic takes up any relief pattern on the master underneath. The plastic is then quickly cooled and a permanent copy of the master is obtained in the plastic.

This process is based on a method of 'blister packaging' so that the basic technology is not specific to Braille production.

Many printing houses have relatively large-scale vacuum-forming units which have either been specially developed for them or are industrial machines which have been modified. There are, however, two companies which produce machines specially for smaller scale Braille copying—namely the American Thermoform Corporation, United States (Appendix B 2), and F. Kutschera & Co., Federal Republic of Germany (Appendix B 2).

With regard to plastic, this can be obtained from specialist suppliers such as: American Thermoform Corporation, Braas & Co. GmbH (Federal Republic of Germany (see Appendix B 2), and Helly-Hansen (Norway—see Appendix B 2).

It is likely that savings can be made if local suppliers are found, although this may imply a poorer quality of less appropriate plastic. Thickness of plastic usually is between 0.1–0.15 mm.

Braille page-scanner

A Braille duplicator which does not conform to the opening remarks of this section is that developed by Micronex Limited (Appendix B 2). They have developed, in conjunction with the RNIB, a scanning machine (Braille Card Scanner, BCS) which optically reads a page embossed (on one side only) with Braille characters. It takes three to five minutes to scan each page and the information is transmitted to a magnetic cassette which can then be used to control an automated Braille embossing device.

Micronex Ltd. describe the current status of their development as follows:

The Braille Card Scanner . . . represents an attempt to produce a card scanner which could be developed within a modest budget and then produced at a cost level consistent with the current-generation data processing equipment. These objectives have been achieved. The system (demonstrated at RNIB in October 1978) is the first of two pre-production systems. The system has been fully developed but is undergoing evaluation in a production environment at RNIB so that we can assess its performance before reaching any conclusions about this particular solution/configuration.[5]

Micronex have also developed a Braille Display and Editing Terminal which can be used to edit the Braille pages scanned by the BCS.

Equipment for the production of Braille

The process of producing Braille material for distribution involves a number of stages, and these can vary depending on the type of production system used. In describing the equipment currently available for Braille production, these various stages (Fig. 1) in the production process will be used as a structure.

Input forms

There are essentially three distinct methods of inputting text into a Braille production system: manual Braille transcribing, manual print encoding, and machine-reading of digitally encoded material.

One of the main justifications for the continuing emphasis in research and development on computer translation of Braille has been the shortage of Braille transcribers. There are, however, certain features associated with manual transcription of Braille that have considerable potential for exploitation, and, in the process, possibly help to attract more people to become transcribers. These advantageous features are masked to a certain extent, at the present time, by the equipment transcribers have to use.

Increasing the speed of operation of keyboards for ordinary commercial use has received extensive attention, certain aspects of which are relevant to Braille. For example, it has been found that: the use of 'chord' keyboards allow entry rates of 150 per cent of standard typing;[6] and 'the act of encoding during a data entry task need not slow down the rate of entry'[7] and '(the process of substituting shortened coded forms for fully spelt text) can be carried on while typing without slowing the keystroke rate', thus implying an increase in entry rate proportional to the decrease in number of keystrokes necessary as a result of the code system.[8]

These findings have not been implemented for general use because the costs involved in retraining staff to use a different keyboard and to learn some coded system for a shortened form of language would not be justified by any savings due to the increased speed, at least in the short term. These factors do not apply, however, when considering Braille transcribing. Chord keyboards are already standard as is a coding system (i.e. contractions) for reducing the number of keystrokes necessary to write any given text.

Until recently, however, the equipment used by transcribers did not take advantage of these factors. Mechanical keyboards were used which are relatively heavy and slow to operate rather than electronic ones. Furthermore the rules involved with writing Braille are in many cases too complex to allow the full benefits of a shortened language form to be taken advantage of.

Some recent developments, for example the introduction of Braille encoding units, at the Braille printing houses in Stockholm and London should show whether the above experimental findings are confirmed in practice.

In general, two main implications arise regarding future development: to design improved Braille keyboards that keep the advantages of chord keyboards, but which are faster and more comfortable to operate than the existing mechanical Braille keyboards; and to investigate the training situation of Braille transcribers so as to optimize the process of learning the Braille code.

The two different types of equipment used for Braille transcribing will be considered separately. Those for mechanical Braille transcribing, which will be discussed under the headings 'Braillewriters and Stereotyping Machines'; and those for 'Manual Braille Encoding'.

Braillewriters and stereotyping machines

Braillewriters have already been described. As stated above, the Perkins is the most widely used machine. In the context of production of Braille for distribution, its disadvantage of not being able to write on both sides of the paper is not so significant. This is because the only effective means of copying Braille sheets can only function with single-sided Braille (see Braille Duplicating). Thus, the advantages of the Perkins machine in terms of its ergonomic design compared with other machines are probably the dominating factors for its widespread use.

Other Braillewriters are available, however, from a number of different countries, namely: the Stainsby Braillewriter (United Kingdon); the Marburg Braillewriter (Federal Republic of Germany); Kong Braillewriter (Republic of Korea); 'Light' Braillewriter (Japan); and Lavendar Braillewriter (United States). Finally, IBM produce a Braillewriter based on their standard Model 'D' typewriter and modified so that the characters on the typearms have Braille characters instead of the normal inkprint characters.

Instead of writing Braille directly on to paper, stereotyping machines emboss the Braille characters into double metal sheets. These sheets can be embossed on both sides thus allowing interpoint and/or interline Braille to be produced. The position of the plate is turned such that the dots of the second side do not interfere with the dots on the first.

Stereotyping machines are heavy-duty machines built for dependability and long life. Details in which machines differ include whether the embossing plate is vertical or horizontal (vertically loaded plates can be more straightforward to set in and take out of the machine), plate size, and whether a one-handed keyboard is available. Availability of the various stereotyping machines is given in Appendix B 3(a).

A range of plates of widely differing sizes, thickness and metal composition is in common use. Plates, ready-cut, folded and punched can probably best be obtained by contacting large Braille printing houses, especially in the case of relatively small users.

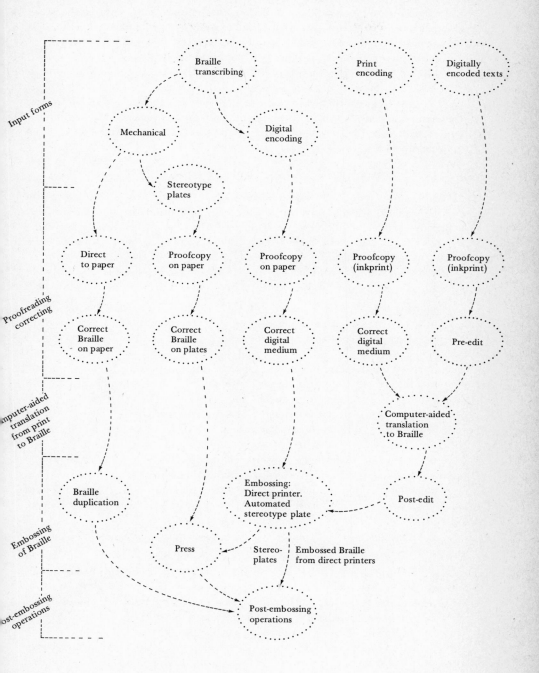

Fig. 1. Stages in different Braille production processes

If local supplies of metal can be found, then equipment will be required to cut the metal sheets to the correct shape, and for folding sheets ready for being embossed. If local suppliers of metal are used, it should be checked first that the metal is of appropriate hardness—if it is too hard the stereotype machine will not be able to emboss dots very effectively; if it is too soft, the plates will only be able to produce a few copies before the dots become flattened by the press.

With regard to costs, this will of course depend on a great number of factors: whether plates are ready cut, type of metal, amount bought, etc. Plate metal is, however, usually bought by weight and a single zinc place, 0.25 mm thick, weighs approximately 0.3 kgs.

Manual Braille encoding

A number of countries have developed Braille writing equipment which allows the capture of Braille characters on some machine-readable medium. In their simplest form Braille encoding equipment need only consist of a six-key Braille keyboard (assuming skilled Braille transcribers already used to such a keyboard layout are to be the operators) and a device for recording the information from the keyboard on to some machine-readable medium. In practice the devices available also provide facilities for correcting the Braille written. These devices are described below.

Loeber modified keypunch. Loeber has modified IBM keypunches so that it is possible to write contracted Braille.[9] This is done from a keyboard similar to that used on ordinary typewriters. From this operation, the Braille is encoded on to punched cards.

The operator then puts the punched card into the machine again. This time the machine reads the cards and prints out the contents of the cards in Braille on a sheet of paper for proofing. The operator checks the accuracy and format of the Braille embossed output and corrects the punched card if an error exists. These cards can then be used to control an automated stereotype machine or similar Braille output device.

As Loeber states, 'While more modern technology is now available, this simple technique of producing master plates with a modified keypunch is a possible solution for locations that do not have access to more elaborate equipment.'[10] Such a system was introduced to the Lutheran Braille Workers, Inc., in 1956 and has proved very satisfactory.

Triformation Perkins Braille Control Electronics (PBCE) (Appendix B 3(b)). Triformation Systems Inc. in the United States produce their own small-scale production system based on a Perkins Brailler. The system consists of: (a) a standard Perkins Braillewriter, slightly modified so that depression of the keys causes electrical impulses to be fed to (b) a Triformation PBCE which codes the keystrokes of the Braillist on to (c) a digital cassette tape recorder, which can play back the data into a (d) Triformation LED-120 Braille page embosser or similar type of Braille output device.

Thus, one line of text is entered from the Perkins into the PBCE memory. By use of a back-space key, characters can be deleted which afford elementary edit/correction ability. One full line of characters (forty) is then transmitted to a storage device. This forms a complete input system in itself so that, in principle, any of the available Braille output devices, or more sophisticated editing facilities such as available with computers, could form the next stage of the production process.

Although the PBCE offers the advantage of writing on to magnetic cassettes, thereby facilitating more convenient and economical long-term storage and easier production of subsequent copies, its improvements over the existing mechanical systems are limited as it still utilizes the Perkins Braillewriter for the keyboard input. Many transcribers who use the Perkins for long periods of time continuously report the keyboard as tiring and heavy to use.

A similar configuration of equipment has been developed at Stiftung Rehabilitation, Heidelberg. The German Braille printing houses did not accept it for production however, due to the large pressure required to operate the Perkins keys.

Société d'Applications Générales d'Electricité et de Mécanique (SAGEM) Braille Embosser (Appendix B 3(b)). The French telecommunications company produces a Braille embosser largely based on their inkprint terminal. This is a desk-top device about the same size as an electric typewriter. The TEM 8BR model is equiped with a standard typewriter keyboard, paper-tape punch and reader, and embossing head. The operation of the keyboard causes the text to be encoded in paper tape simultaneously with the embossing of Braille paper.

All sixty-four Braille characters can be produced by single keys from the keyboard. Alternatively, it is possible to have an option that allows this same keyboard to be operated as a 6-key 'chord' keyboard. That is to say, that only six keys (and the space bar) are active on the keyboard and these keys then function in an analogous way to the Perkins keyboard. Thus, a TEM 8BR unit with paper-tape reader and punch can function as an independent production unit or as input to some other digitally controlled output device.

Text-editing machine for Braille (see Appendix B 3(b)). As part of a large research and development programme on the rationalization of Braille printing techniques[11] carried out by Stiftung Rehabilitation, a text-editing machine for Braille was developed. A second generation of this machine is now under construction and is to be introduced into German Braille printing houses.

This equipment has a six-key Braille keyboard plus space and control keys interfaced by microprocessor to electronic storage capable of holding one page of characters. Operation of the keyboard displays the characters that have been keyed. Both a visual display (a line of forty-eight 4×2 light emitting diodes) and a Braille display (a line of 8-dot Braille display modules) are incorporated in the equipment, thus allowing both sighted and visually handicapped transcribers to use it.[12]

When using this machine, one line of Braille is written at a time and stored in a buffer memory; it can be checked via one of the displays. The characters in this buffer store can be corrected, removed or new ones inserted; thus a total page can be corrected and proof-read line by line as often as necessary. When the line is correct it is transmitted to punched paper tape or compact cassettes (according to ECMA34 standard).

RNIB (London) Braille encoding unit (Braille-Cassette-Terminal, BCT). These Braille cassette encoders were specially developed by Sigma Electronic Systems (Appendix B 3(b)) for the RNIB and were introduced into the new RNIB production system during autumn 1978.

These devices consist of a six-key Braille keyboard plus space bar and control keys, a cassette (write only) machine and a six-line visual display showing the Braille characters in dot form. These devices were developed as direct replacements for RNIB manual stereotyping machines and so mostly they will be used for books and magazines for multiple copy production.

During transcribing, the text fills the visual display; when this becomes full (at the end of the sixth line), the text is transmitted automatically over to the cassette so that the visual display always shows the last six lines written. This text which is visible is available for correcting or inserting new characters at any time.

Once the text is encoded on the tape it cannot be read back into the display. Furthermore, once a cassette has been taken out of the machine, or the machine switched off, the same cassette cannot be set in the machine again; a new cassette must be taken. This means that a job encoded on to a number of unfilled cassettes must be merged together on to new cassette(s) before being read into the central computer. The original cassettes can then be erased and reused.

SRF's Braille encoding units, Sweden. These devices are based on standard equipment, in common use in newspaper and book-printing houses in Sweden, manufactured by Tele-ekonomi AB (see Appendix B 3(b)). They were introduced into SRF's Braille production system during spring 1978.

The encoding units consist of a six-key Braille keyboard, a visual display unit showing up to twenty-four lines and a cassette (read/write) machine. The visual-display unit has an internal memory corresponding to approximately five pages of Braille. The text in this internal memory is available at any time for correcting and re-doing the format. The text is displayed in alphabetic and some special symbols. There is one, and one only, visual character for each Braille character so that the text format displayed on the visual-display screen corresponds exactly to the eventual Braille format. When the internal memory is full, this is signalled and the text is encoded on to cassette, and transcribing then continues.

Before transcribing is begun, the cassette machine searches for 'workspace' on the tape, i.e. it searches for the last character encoded on the tape, then winds the tape forward a certain distance so that there is a gap between the previous text and the new text to be transcribed. This gap also functions as a 'stop' instruction to the cassette machines used for reading the encoded text.

The equipment is microprocessor based, so considerable flexibility is possible. For example, a keyboard based on a standard typewriter layout (QWERTY) can be substituted for the Braille keyboard; the full Swedish contracted code system can be written using this keyboard. Also, a forty-character eight-dot Braille display can be interfaced to the encoding unit. This allows visually handicapped transcribers to use the equipment.

Manual print encoding

For languages where there exist translation programmes for Braille, inkprint text can be written into the translation system. There are three main ways of doing this manually: de-centralized, centralized, and using a service bureau.

De-centralized encoding equipment

Which equipment is used can depend on the local environment—e.g. the media used by the computer system, the best equipment offered by the local manufacturers' agents, costs, etc. Such equipment is essentially standard equipment requiring no major modifications, although the code generated may require some modification in some cases.

As part of the Stiftung Rehabilitation research programme,[13] a detailed market study was carried out of de-centralized text-encoding equipment for input to a computerized Braille translation system, including paper-tape perforators, data terminals, optical character recognition (OCR) typewriters, and text-processors. The criteria used for evaluating these devices were: correcting facilities; whether the special German characters (ü, ä, ö, ß) were available; compatibility of equipment with computer systems, i.e. could the encoded text be converted to standard computer readable form; ease of handling of the recording medium; portability of equipment; and costs.

Centralized terminals

If encoding is to be carried out on the premises of the printing house, then terminals linked directly into the computer can be used. Again, these terminals can be completely standard and in most cases choice of these terminals can be made in conjunction with the choice of the computer to be used for translation.

Service bureau

In many countries there now exist service bureaux which can be used for the encoding of text and also for translation if supplied with the suitable translation programme. With this alternative, the printing house avoids the investment and running costs of having such equipment on their premises. Careful costing should be made, however, as to whether money is saved in the long run as service bureaux can be expensive.

Furthermore, most Braille translation programmes require some 'help' when translating certain parts of texts, such as abbreviations, italics, capital letters, etc.; these must be indicated by the person encoding the text. The use of such indicators in the text can be learnt by operators quite easily if they work with such material all the time. Books going out to a service bureau must be well marked beforehand, however, as they could be encoded by someone unfamiliar with such texts.

Digitally encoded texts

An increasing variety of texts and information is becoming available on machine-readable media. It is possible, therefore, to read this material directly into a Braille translation system, thereby eliminating the need to re-write material which has already been written by someone else. Such material ranges from compositors' tapes

(tapes used for automated phototypesetting of inkprint books) to information stored in data banks, such as references to, and abstracts of, academic publications.

The process of converting compositors' tapes to a form suitable for reading into a Braille translation system is not straightforward. These tapes contain many special codes which are used for controlling the photo-typesetting equipment, and they often contain many errors, both those from the first encoding of the text and omissions of subsequent alterations which are normally done manually on the print output and not on the tape. Thus, a pre-editing stage is necessary before translation can begin. Although a certain amount of this editing can be done automatically by the computer, an efficient system also really requires some interactive capability.[14]

With regard to equipment, nothing specific for Braille is required other than interactive capability. On the other hand, it would be necessary to develop programmes to convert the different printers' codes to the one used by the translation system and, perhaps, other programmes to assist with the more specialized aspects of Braille editing and layout. In other words, such a system requires specialized computer personnel closely familiar with details of Braille and its production to develop the system.

Proof-reading and correction

Material transcribed directly into Braille

From Braillewriters
Material written on a mechanical Braillewriter can be used directly for proof-reading. The errors can be marked on the paper (e.g. by a dot or other mark in the margin opposite the line which contains the error) and/or a report can be written saying which lines (page number and line number are usually given) contain errors, what the errors are and what should be written instead.

Proof-reading is often carried out by visually handicapped persons who are experienced Braille readers. Certain types of errors, however, require reference to the original text, e.g. where there are numbers. This means that there must be sighted people available in order to check with the original text. More complex texts are usually proof-read by two people, one reading the Braille text and the other checking the original text visually.

Small errors can be corrected by pressing down the characters which are incorrect,[15] then writing out the correct character(s) using a slate and stylus. If larger amounts of text need to be corrected or inserted, then the whole page or several pages may need to be totally rewritten so that the inserted text can be fitted in.

From stereotyping machines
Braille written on to stereotype plates can be read directly from the plates. However, it is preferable to take a proof-copy from the plates on paper. This can be done in an ordinary hand-operated platen press or equivalent. This paper copy can be proof-read by the same methods described above.

Correcting, however, must be made to the metal plates. This usually means hammering down the characters with a blunt stylus, then putting the plate back in the stereotype machine and writing the correct characters. Or, as with mechanical Braillewriters, larger errors can mean the re-writing of a whole, or several, plates. The correcting tools can normally be bought from the stereotype manufacturer together with the stereotype machine.

From Braille encoding units
If Braille is first encoded on to a machine-readable medium, this can be used to run off a proof copy from a Braille printer, or in both English and Swedish systems (see Manual Braille Encoding) coded print proof copy can also be produced if required.

The advantage of encoding text is that sophisticated text-processing techniques can be employed to correct the text. This results in an error-free cassette, paper-tape or similar, which can then be used for production of stereotype plates or Braille on paper which do not need to be proof-read.

The printer used for producing proof copy needs to be fast, but quality of Braille is a less critical factor (although this would be more important if the printer is going to be used for production as well).

The equipment used at RNIB in London are on-line text-editing machines specially developed by Sigma Electronics (see Appendix B 3(b). These terminals display a complete Braille page in dot patterns and have full text-editing facilities.

The equipment used at the SRF in Stockholm is based on standard Tele-ekonomi equipment (see Appendix B 3(b)) and consists of a visual-display unit, keyboard and two cassette machines—one for reading in the uncorrected text and the other for recording the corrected text. The equipment is microprocessor-based and has full text-editing facilities. The text-editing equipment developed at Stiftung Rehabilitation can also be used in this context.

Material encoded in print
It is usual with key-punching of text to 'verify' the first encoding by another person writing the same text, then comparing the two encoded texts automatically—where they do not match exactly a mistake is present in one of the texts, assuming that it is unlikely for two people to make the same mistake in the same place. Verification can be expected to reduce the errors in the encoded text from between 2 and 5 per cent after the first encoding to a neglible amount. The disadvantage with this method is that it requires the text to be written twice, which means considerable extra cost, especially if being done at a commercial service bureau.

If a text-processor is used for the text preparation, the operators can check and correct their own output. The correcting facilities now incorporated in these machines are quite sophisticated so this can be quite an effective means of text preparation, especially in the context of a de-centralized input system.

On-line terminals usually allow full text correcting and editing facilities. Hard-copy output can also be produced very quickly via on-line, high-speed printers.

The above concerns only those corrections made to the text prior to translation into Braille. In most cases where high-quality Braille is required, a proof-reading and correction/editing stage will also be necessary after translation. The degree to which this will be necessary, however, will depend on a number of factors, such as the amount of marking up of special features in the text before encoding, the quality of Braille required and the quality of the programme. This latter aspect should be constantly improved and updated, however, as more experience is gained with regard to its shortcomings.

Digitally encoded texts

Text obtained in digital form for book production must undergo both a pre- and post-editing stage. First, the tapes must be converted from the typesetter's code to the code used by the Braille translation system. Also, certain special instruction codes, only relevant to the production of inkprint, must be removed. This can be achieved automatically.

The result of this preliminary processing is then proof-read and corrected, preferably interactively, on an on-line terminal. The extent of this pre-editing of the text will depend on the quality of Braille required and will, almost certainly, be a compromise between this and the time (and cost) available for production.

When this stage is complete, translation can be carried out, followed by a further editing stage for insertion of contents pages, page references, etc. The efficiency of these editing procedures will be a critical factor in whether such tapes can be effectively utilized for Braille production.[16]

Computer-aided translation of print to Braille

The first translation programme for grade II Braille was developed in the late 1950s by IBM in conjunction with the American Printing House for the Blind. This first programme was written in assembler language and so could not be transferred to other machines.

During the late 1960s programmes were being developed in high-level languages at the University of Münster (Federal Republic of Germany) and the Argonne National Laboratory (United States), using PL/1 and by MITRE Corp. (United States) using COBOL (DOTSYS).

Table-driven programmes in high-level languages (such as DOTSYS III) can be transferred to a range of computers. They are also relatively straightforward to modify to cope with other languages by changing the input 'dictionary' containing the particular Braille system's contractions and their rules. This development means that translation software can be bought and implemented, thus avoiding each country having to develop its own translation programme. DOTSYS III, for example, is available from a number of centres (see Appendix B 3(c)).

In 1975, two of the original developers of the DOTSYS III programme began the further development of this programme which led, in 1976, to the founding of Duxbury Systems Inc. (see Appendix B 3(c)). An improved version of the DOTSYS III programme is now available from Duxbury Systems and they have now developed tables for British Braille.

Duxbury Systems also offer complete production systems to run on 'any Data General NOVA or ECLIPSE or Digital Equipment "11" series computer with FORTRAN support and at least 25K words of memory (plus operating system).'[17] If other equipment is preferred by the customer, conversion can be specially quoted.

American Systems Inc. also provides automated Braille translation systems. Complete systems, however, must be bought, including both equipment and the programmes.[18]

A considerable amount of work has also been carried out in Europe in this area. A translation programme for German was developed in 1967–68 at the University of Münster (Appendix B 3(c)). This programme is written in PL/1 and is now in use in Heidelberg,[19] Leipzig[20] and Vienna.[21] During the early 1970s translation programmes were developed for Dutch (Appendix B 3(c)) and for Danish (Appendix B 3(c)). In France a grade II programme for French has been developed at the Centre Tobia (Appendix B 3(c)) and by Charpentier (Appendix B 3(c)). Centre Tobia has also carried out some work on a grade II Spanish translator, but this was stopped due to changes being made in the Spanish code system.[22]

In Canada (Appendix B 3(c)) a new approach to translation has been developed which can handle French, English and bilingual French/English texts. The basic strategy is to divide the text up into its component words, gather all occurrences of a given form into adjacent positions in the file, and then translate each different form once, substituting for all occurrences of the form, and then re-sort the material into text order for final formatting.[23]

Other more sophisticated alternatives to the table-driven programmes are also being researched by Coleman who is investigating the possibilities of applying a 'structured programming' approach to translators.[24]. Also, at the University of Münster the application of Markov algorithms is being investigated.[25]

With the very significant developments in microprocessors in recent years, these are now being used for Braille translation. Such work is being carried out in Singapore (Appendix B 3(c)), Stockholm (Appendix B 3(c)) and the University of Münster (see Appendix B 3(c) in direct connection with the Braille printing houses there).[26]

Although full documentation is available on most of these translation programmes, their implementation would largely be the responsibility of the user, and therefore, require the close involvement of a computer specialist. The process of automated translation involves more than just the actual conversion of the inkprint characters to their corresponding Braille characters. There must also be facilities for formatting and editing the Braille text. Furthermore, manual pre- and/or post-editing of the text may be necessary in order to get the highest quality of Braille book.

The introduction of a computer-aided translation system is, therefore, a relatively complex undertaking and expert advice and involvement should be sought. There exist two main sources of information on computerized Braille translation: the 'Sub-committee on Computerised Braille Production and Other Media' and the Warwick Research Unit for the Blind (WRUB). The former consists of D. W. Croisdale (Chairman) (Appendix B 3(c)), R. A. J. Gildea (Appendix B 3(c)) and Professor

H. Werner (Appendix B 3(c)) and has defined for itself a number of specific objectives. These are:

to create and maintain an international directory of people and organisations involved or interested in computerised Braille production; to collect and disseminate information of a statistical nature about current production systems and future plans; to hold international meetings to help achieve the aims.[27]

The latter research unit (Appendix B 3(c)) produces an *International Register of Research on Blindness and Visual Impairment* and an occasional journal *Braille Research Newsletter* in conjunction with the American Foundation for the Blind.

Braille embossing equipment

When discussing embossing devices, it is useful to distinguish between two different types. There are *parallel* embossers, i.e. devices which produce one page (or more commonly, a double page) in as many copies as are needed, followed by all the copies of the next page and so on until the edition is complete. Braille production from stereotype plates is an example of this type of output. In contrast there are *sequential* embossers which produce one complete copy of the transcribed material at a time. Thus, if multiple copies are required the Braille-encoded medium controlling the output device can be run through the printer as many times as the number of copies required. All devices of this type are controlled from a coding medium such as paper tape or magnetic cassette.

These two types of embossers show a different relationship between their output time and the variables, numbers of pages and numbers of copies. This can be shown symbolically as follows:

Output time for a parallel embosser = $N \cdot R_p + N \cdot n \cdot t_p$

> where: N = number of pages
> n = number of copies
> R_p = resetting time for embosser (i.e. time between pages)
> t_p = time to emboss a single page

Output time for a sequential embosser = $n \cdot R_s + N \cdot n \cdot t_s$

> where: N, n as above
> R_s = resetting time for embosser (i.e. time beween copies)
> t_s = time to emboss a single page

How these two equations relate to production time and number of copies is illustrated in Figure 2.

Figure 2 shows that production time with sequential embossers is much more sensitive to the number of copies produced than are parallel embossers. In view of the fact that Braille production system often has to cope with production of small runs, the plotting of a diagram similar to Figure 2 for specific printers can be very helpful in deciding the type of printer a particular printing house requires.

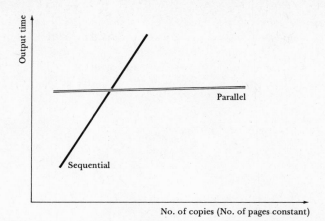

Fig. 2. Graph illustrating the different relationships of production time to number of copies produced for sequential and parallel embossers.

Sequential embossers

SAGEM Braille printer (Appendix B 3(b))

SAGEM Braille printers have been discussed above, in particular the TEM 8BR model which consists of a keyboard and printer unit. There is also available a model without a keyboard (Model REM 8BR) which can be bought with a paper-tape reader; alternatively, it can be interfaced to any suitable digital device or computer. Its speed as a production machine is rather slow—15 characters/second; it is, however, capable of producing interpoint Braille and the quality is generally regarded as being good.

Triformation printers (Appendix B 3(b)

Triformation Systems Inc. is an American company specializing in producing a variety of Braille-related products. Their fastest printer is the LED-120 which can print 40-character Braille lines on fan-fold, continuous paper at 180 lines per minute (i.e. 120 characters/second).

There were over thirty of these machines in use in 1976, most of them in the United States and Canada.[28] There are now, however, several in Europe, including the Dutch Library for the Blind, Warwick Research Unit for the Blind, and RNIB.

Most users report that this machine functions satisfactorily. However, many also emphasize the need to keep the machine regularly maintained and adjusted if it is to function reliably.

Other models available are based on the LED-120. These are the LED-30 (up to 30 characters/second) and the LED-15 (up to 15 characters/second). These are cheaper than the LED-120.

IBM 1403 modified printer (Appendix B 3(d))

This modification is 'an operator interchangeable device that will convert an IBM Model II or 1403 Model N1 Printer from standard printing to Braille printing in less than ten minutes conversion time. This printer will produce Braille output in the form of either simple single-run throw-away copy or permanent textbook-type copy. The IBM 1403 N1 printer can produce up to 19,000 Braille characters/minute (366 Braille lines/minute). The 1403 Model II printer can produce up to 10,400 Braille characters/minute (200 Braille lines/minute)'.[29]

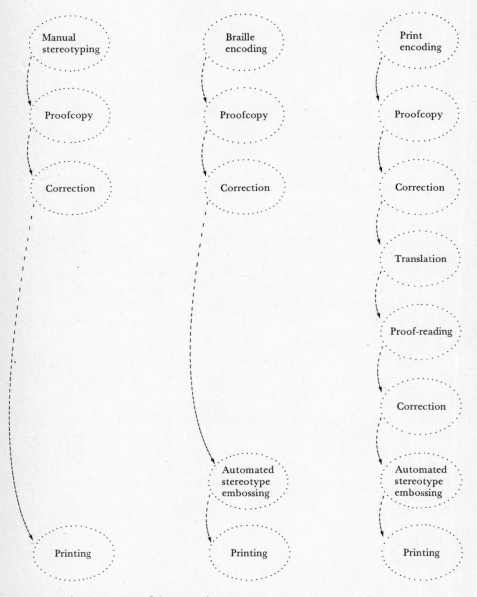

Fig. 3.   Production stages of three production systems.

This type of printer is used by the Danish Braille Printing House (Appendix B 3(c)) and by Stiftung Rehabilitation, Heidelberg (Appendix B 3(c)).

Parallel embossing

Braille printing from stereotype plates

The automated embossing of stereotype plates forms an extra process preceding the 'parallel' output of braille from a press. Consider the stages of three different production systems.

In the entirely manual system (to the left in Fig. 3) there are just four stages from transcribing the text to printing Braille. In the case of electronic coding of Braille (in the centre of Fig. 3) there is an extra stage—that of automated embossing of plates. In the case of encoding print, then translating this to Braille by computer there can be four stages more than necessary with direct manual stereotyping. The effective organization of these extra stages is an important factor in whether the modern systems will in fact function more efficiently than the traditional methods.

It is in fact quite likely that short-length material (two to three pages for example) required in multiple copies can be produced more quickly manually on a stereotype machine than through a computerized system. The electronic methods, however, show their advantages of having more flexible correction procedures when producing longer material, such as books.

Nevertheless, Figure 3 illustrates that a slow, automated stereotyping machine could easily produce a severe bottleneck in the system using digital encoding methods for input. This would cause the under-utilization of the input facilities which, as they represent a large capital investment, would mean that production costs would be unnecessarily high.

This was in fact a real danger when Braille printing houses began introducing electronic equipment, converting their existing manual stereotyping machines to run automatically. Thus, American Printing House, RNIB and Marburg converted their stereotype machines in this way. These machines are, however, only capable of a slow speed—4 to 5 characters/second. Even with a number of such stereotypes, the embossing capacity at present can be the limiting factor in a printing house's capacity.

There are now becoming available, however, plate-embossing machines which have been purpose built for running from digital media and are significantly faster than the machines converted from manual operation.

Marburg automated stereotype. Developed as part of the Stiftung Rehabilitation project, this stereotype machine is described in the Final Report from that project as follows:

[The] data controlled stereotyper . . . can emboss Braille characters stored in digital form on data-carriers onto double-layered zinc, aluminium or tin-plate sheeting at a speed of 10 characters per second. We were able to achieve the high-speed character embossing which moves the zinc sheet thanks to a new method of fixing the stencil, which makes it unnecessary to have a frame to hold the sheet. In this way, we were able to reduce the mass which has to be accelerated and stopped with this great frequency character by character to less than 1000 g. . . .

It is constructed as a table-top machine, connected to a control unit by sheathed cables. The control unit contains all the power-supply units and switching elements necessary for the control and operation of the machine, and the reader for the data-carrier.[30]

Triformation PED-30 plate embosser. In 1978 Triformation Systems Inc. produced a plate-embossing device capable of 30 characters per second. 'Interfaced with a computer or other coded information source, the PED-30 accumulates data in its buffer which has a capacity of 2048 characters. As the buffer receives information it relays it to the mechanical device which embosses the double-folded metal plate at a rate of 30 Braille characters per second. At the end of a page, the plate is manually turned and the process repeated.'[31]

The first complete machine is currently in use at the Clovernook Printing House, United States (Appendix A 45). According to the manufacturers, the PED-30 can turn out thirty-eight plates per hour, whereas the machines it is designed to replace produce about forty plates per day. From these estimates, therefore, the PED-30 represents a very significant increase in embossing capacity without involving any change in the production system.

Braille presses
Braille presses are, by and large, standard machines which have been modified to take account of the fact that the paper must be embossed rather than printed. There is a considerable range of presses in use for Braille production, as Table 1 below illustrates.

Table 1. Braille printing presses in use in some printing houses around the world

Printing house	Equipment description	Speed	Type of production used for
Clovernook (Appendix A 45)	Flat-bed presses of own design printing from rolls of about 400 lb.	16,000 pages/hour	—
	Automatic flat-bed presses	8,000 pages/hour	Title pages.
	Hand-fed flat-bed presses	2,000 pages/hour	—
Scottish Braille Press (Appendix A 44)	Hamilton flat-bed press, hand-fed	540 pages/hour	General and specialized books in interpoint.
	Timson rotary press	9,000–10,000 pages/hour	Pamphlets and weekly, monthly and quarterly magazines.
Howe Press (Appendix A 45)	Converted cardboard box cutter (platen press)	—	General and specialized books, pamphlets, and monthly and quarterly magazines in interpoint.
	Antique converted cylinder letter presses	—	

Association Valentin Haüy (Appendix A 12)	Hydraulic flat-bed press	2,500–3,600 pages/hour	—
Iran (Appendix A 20)	Heidelberg press, Marburg press	500 pages/hour	Specialized books and monthly magazines in interpoint.
Barcelona (Appendix A 37)	Minerva Victoria platen press (Federal Republic of Germany) Minerva Seroglia platen press (Italy) Rotary press (Federal Republic of Germany)	4,000 pages/hour 4,800 pages/hour 40,000 pages/ hour	General and specialized books, pamphlets and monthly, quarterly and less frequently published magazines in interpoint.
Madrid (Appendix A 37)	Hercules Barcina stamping machine (platen press) by Gutenberg S.A. Planeta Minerva platen press Rotary press by Blind. Studieanstalt, Marburg Ordered a Roto-folio II from König and Bauer (Federal Republic of Germany)	800–1,300 strokes/hour 3,000 pages/hour 4,000 pages/hour —	General and specialized books, pamphlets and monthly, quarterly and less frequently published magazines in interpoint. Magazines only. —
Saudi Arabia (Appendix A 34)	Victoria press	—	General books and pamphlets in interpoint.

As Table 1 shows, the speed of presses used for Braille production varies between a few hundred to 40,000 pages per hour. There is also a variety of types of presses, their main distinguishing characteristic being whether they are flat-bed or rotary presses. The majority of presses in use appear to be platen presses, which some people maintain give better quality Braille than a rotary press. The main advantage of rotary presses would seem to lie in their high speed of operation.

As Braille presses are more or less standard machines, no comprehensive list of manufacturers will be included. Direct contact with local manufacturers or manufacturers' agents is suggested as the best way of initiating any market survey, as it is a very great advantage if there are local service and maintenance facilities. If this is not possible, however, then contact can be made with the printing houses listed in Appendix A.

Braille embossers under development

In 1979 there were a number of Braille embossers in an advanced stage of development. It is not yet clear, however, whether these will become commercially available; thus no reliable information with regard to costs and conditions of sale can be given.

Sequential embossers

The *SINTEF interpoint Braille printer* exists in prototype form and has been successfully in use at a school for the blind in Tambartum, Norway. This printer embosses Braille simultaneously on both sides of the paper at approximately 100 characters per second or one sheet of paper embossed on both sides in 20 seconds. This speed is expected to be at least doubled in the next version of the printer. See Appendix B 3(f).

The *Thiel brailler* was designed and a prototype built at the Laboratory of Fine Mechanics of the Mechanical Engineering Department of Delft University of Technology, the Netherlands.[32] The commercial development of this brailler was taken over by Thiel GmbH (see Appendix B 3(f)) and a production prototype was successfully exhibited at a congress in Heidelberg in October 1978. Prototypes have been installed and are working, and the printer is now available for purchase.

Parallel embossers

A prototype of the *Zoltan Braille embosser* has been constructed at Trask Datasystem AB in Stockholm. Its design is based on a rotary-press principle, but instead of placing an embossed plate around the drums, embossing pins, which can be set in embossing or non-embossing positions, are located in the drums themselves. Thus, once all these pins are set (this can be done from a computer or some digitally-coded medium), the embosser functions as a high-speed rotary press (see Appendix B 3(f)). A project to evaluate this embosser from a technical point of view and to determine the market potential for such an embosser was carried out in spring/summer 1979.

A *rotary Braille printer* similar to the Zoltan has also been developed in Sweden by L.-E. Andersson (see Appendix B 3(f)), intended for manual and smaller-scale production than the Zoltan. This machine has a Braille keyboard by which pins can be magnetically set into two drums, each of which corresponds to one side of an interpoint Braille page. When both drums are set the required number of copies can be run off by passing paper between the rotating drums. When this is completed the next two pages can be written.

Post-embossing operations

Before looking at gathering Braille sheets after embossing, sorting them into their correct sequence, and binding the material into book or magazine form, it may be useful to discuss briefly some of the variables existing at the Braille printing stage which are relevant to the subsequent post-embossing stages.

Some preliminary aspects of post-embossing operations

Page size

The dimensions of the paper used for Braille material is commonly larger than that used for equivalent inkprint material and there is no standard size of Braille page in use internationally. There is a trend, however, towards the standardization of paper sizes for general use. This is the DIN standard which is illustrated by Figure 4.

The increasing acceptance of this standard generally means that all machinery

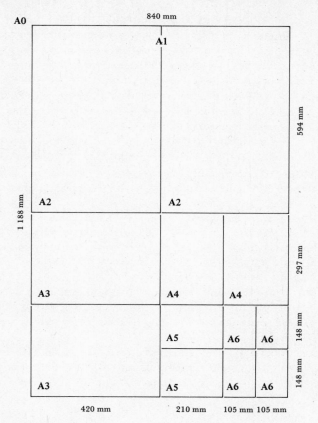

Fig. 4.   DIN standard of paper sizes.

and equipment relating to paper handling will be designed to suit these standard dimensions. This goes beyond just actual paper size, and paper-handling equipment, as sizes of files, folders, envelopes, etc., will also gradually be adapted to this standard.

Much of this standard equipment can be used for Braille so it is therefore an advantage if the sizes of Braille sheets also conform to these increasingly standard dimensions. This will maximize the availability of equipment and minimize costs by avoiding unnecessary 'special modifications' to accommodate Braille sheet sizes.

Type of output from Braille printers and presses
There are a number of different ways Braille sheets can arrive from the printing department to the post-embossing department. They can be single sheets or fan-folded, continuous sheets; they can be stacks of uncollated sheets from a 'parallel' output or complete copies of the book or equivalent from a 'sequential' output; they can be embossed on one side or on both sides. These factors naturally have implications for post-embossing equipment and methods.

In general, multiple copy material is printed in 'parallel' on double sheets (A3 or similar). These are then gathered, stitched and folded. The techniques used for this type of material cannot, in general, be used for output from mechanical Braille-writers, vacuum-forming, or 'sequential' Braille printers, or vice versa. Output from these devices is produced in single sheets (A4 or similar) which then must be bound or glued or, for some material, can be punched and set into a loose-leaf folder.

In the case of computer-controlled sequential output on fan-folded paper, considerable savings on post-embossing operations can be made by printing every even numbered page upside-down. This means that the sheets, in fan-folded form, can be cut directly and the sheets will be ready gathered in their correct sequence. The Danish Braille Printing House (Appendix A 10) uses this technique with their IBM 1403 Braille printer. After cutting the sheets on three sides, they set them directly in a ring binder such that the Braille appears on both the left and right sides of the ring binding as if it was interpoint Braille.

The IBM 1403 printer only produces single-sided Braille. For interpoint Braille printers, such as the SAGEM (which prints all the odd-numbered pages first, then the paper is turned and reinserted and all the even pages are printed), the embossed sheets can be fed through a 'burster' so that the sheets stack in their correct sequence ready for binding (see Appendix B 3(g)).[33]

In the case of the printer being developed in Norway (Appendix B 3(f)(i)), a slightly more complex rearrangement of the printing cycle used by the Danish Printing House can be used so as the Braille sheets are in their correct sequence after embossing.

In general, therefore, 'parallel' output of Braille requires a gathering operation before binding. With 'sequential' output, the output can be gathered in the correct sequence and thus can go direct to binding.

Gathering[34]

There is considerably greater conformity on how Braille sheets are gathered, ready for binding, than there is on how it is printed or bound. That is, it is done mainly by hand. There appear to be only three printing houses with automated facilities for this operation. Two of these, the Scottish Braille Press and the American Printing House for the Blind, use the same equipment—a Hobson collating, folding and wire-stitching machine (Appendix B 3(g)). In addition, RNIB used to use a Macey saddle stitcher for collating and stitching the ready folded sheets from their Solid Dot production. With RNIB's new system, the Solid Dot system is no longer to be used and they have developed an automated system which prints Braille from twelve stereotype plates simultaneously, gathers, stitches and folds the sheets in one continuous process.

With regard to the Hobson suction-fed collator, this is standard equipment, modified slightly for operation with Braille sheets. When using ordinary printed paper, the sheets will slide over each other quite easily. This is not the case when embossed sheets are used and therefore the paper feed has to be adjusted so that each sheet is placed exactly during the collating operation, and does not have to slide into position.

An advantage of the Hobson collator over other similar machines is its simple folding mechanism. This is achieved by a bar coming down in the centre of the sheets, thus creating a fold. Other machines (e.g., Harris sidebinder) use a multiple roller system for folding which, although possible, is not so successful for thick embossed paper.

The Hobson collator has a speed of between 1,200 to 4,500 sets per hour. Thus, even at its slowest speeds, not many printing houses for Braille could use such equipment to full capacity. The American Printing House uses its machine for about twenty-five to thirty hours per week and it is, therefore, rather well used. The Scottish Braille Press, on the other hand, uses its machine for a shorter period of time per week. In the latter case, the justification for needing such a high-speed machine is given as follows:

Machinery used is largely determined by the time available between preparation of copy and publication date and this means the need for fast machines which are only in use for a limited number of hours per day. This is particularly so in the case of weekly publications.[35]

The majority of Braille printing houses, however, gather the Braille sheets by hand. A part of the rationale for this is the small scale of production relative to that of ordinary printing houses and perhaps lack of money for investment in mechanical equipment, which in general tends to be rather expensive. There is, however, another aspect to this situation which is well expressed by the following quotation from the Howe Press (United States):

We have found that hand collating has two advantages in Braille production. It is reliable and conducive to high quality work. A person will notice the misprinted sheet, the sheet turned upside down, the wrongly numbered sheet, etc. ... Also, we find collating is a job blind people can do and do well, using their Braille skills checking sheets, etc. ... It is not an exciting career full of potential for creative fulfilment or unlimited advancement, but it is employment, useful and steady.[36]

Whatever one's opinion on whether Braille printing houses have an obligation to employ blind people, they often do function in this way. Consequently, if new methods are introduced despite this situation, or in ignorance of it, as many problems may be created as are solved.

Binding

As for printing equipment, there is a wide range of binding equipment in use in Braille printing houses. This is illustrated by Table 2.

As for other post-embossing equipment, binding techniques for Braille use, by and large, standard equipment. One technique special to Braille, however, is to set thin strips of Braille paper between the embossed sheets such that they lie along the left-hand margin of the sheets. This extra thickness in the bound part of the book is to compensate for the extra thickness of the paper where it has been embossed with Braille. Failure to do this causes the Braille pages to bow upwards when bound so that the covers do not lie flat when the book is closed.

One technique which is becoming increasingly used by Braille printing houses is that of 'spiral binding'. This technique is simple to carry out and can be done on completely mechanical or on electrically-assisted equipment. This type of binding has the advantage of allowing the book to be opened out completely flat and can even be folded back to back without damaging the binding. Details of two systems—Burns 'Wire-O' system and that of the Spiral Binding Co. Inc.—are given in Appendix B 3(g).

A simple binding system for Braille sheets embossed on paper with sprocket-drive holes is that of Velo-bind (see Appendix B 3(g)). This consists of a 'comb-like' arrangement, the teeth of which fit through the sprocket holes, and is then fixed in place.

Table 2.   Binding equipment in current use in some Braille printing houses

Printing house	Description of equipment
Clovernook (Appendix A 45)	Magazines are saddle-stitched with Bostitch wire stapler. Books are bound either with plastic ring binding equipment or metal rings. General binding equipment is used.
Singapore (Appendix A 35)	Brass screws, brass bolts and cardboard folders. NSC plastic binding system, i.e. using plastic spirals also used.
Scottish Braille Press (Appendix A 44)	For general and special books a Martini book-sewing machine is used. These are sewn with Letterfile covers. Magazine material is stitched automatically by the Hobson collator.
Howe Press (Appendix A 45)	For book, metal circela elements are riveted into polyethylene covers. General Binding Corp. element and riveter and Hallenbach hot stamping machine used. Saddle-stitching used for magazines.
Malaysia (Appendix A 25)	Punches and binder from General Binding Corp. are used for ring binding with Cerlex plastic ring binder.
Iran (Appendix A 20)	Recently imported Müller-Martini FD book-sewing machine.
Barcelona and Madrid (Appendix A 37)	Have ordered Martini sewing machines.
India (Appendix A 18)	Morrison book stitcher used for material of less than 100 pages. Larger books or magazines are bound externally by local binders.
Saudia Arabia (Appendix A 34)	Cefmer-Brehmer sewing machine. Polygraph wire-stitching machine.

Factors in the design of Braille production systems

So far in this chapter, only the different elements that can make up a Braille production system have been considered. Naturally, the equipment discussed can be organized in many different ways according to the type of production required. A number of factors should be considered when developing or expanding Braille production facilities. These are as follows:

Size of production

How large is the need for Braille? How many different titles, magazines, etc., are required? In how many copies? Answers to these questions will obviously play a decisive role in the selection of equipment of appropriate capacity.

Type of production

Is the predominant need for books (in small numbers of copies) or for magazine-type material (in relatively large numbers of copies)? How are the needs distributed between school children, material for work requirements, students, and casual reading matter? (See Chapter 2.) How much time is available for the production of the regular magazines? A predominant need for magazine material, requiring production within a tight time schedule, can imply the necessity for selecting equipment for fast production, even though their total capacity is not required. The needs of the various 'market sectors' involve quite different demands on a production system; therefore, these differences should influence the type of equipment chosen and its organization.

Costs

Two aspects should be considered. The initial investment costs of the equipment and the running costs. Money is not always saved by buying the cheapest alternative. Plastic, for example, is significantly more expensive than paper in most countries; paper tape is considerably cheaper to buy than digital cassettes but the latter can be re-used many times.

Technical infrastructure

How well developed technologically is the country introducing the system? Are there companies, organizations, etc., available to develop or interface equipment? Are there companies who are able to service and maintain the equipment? Simple transference of sophisticated equipment can create enormous problems if there is no technical back-up easily available in the country introducing the equipment.

Translation programme

Is there a Braille translation programme available for the language(s) used? Translation programmes exist for English, German, French, Spanish, Danish and Dutch and several more are under development, e.g. Portuguese (Brazil). However, local variations in either the language and/or the Braille code may make some modifications to these translation programme necessary before they can be used in countries other than the one in which they were developed.

Existing resources

Do Braille production facilities already exist? If so, in what respect are they inadequate? How many Braille transcribers are there? How difficult is it to recruit and train new ones? Some countries may already have quite good Braille facilities but still need to expand their production. Others may have very old or inefficient equipment and therefore need to replace it. These represent two quite different starting points for developing a new Braille production system.

Examples of Braille production systems

In order to make the previous discussion on equipment for and design factors in Braille production systems a little more concrete, five different system configurations will be described. Each will be presented in relation to the above design factors.

System I: Large-scale, computerized production system, Largely on-line to central computer (see Fig. 5)

This system allows both Braille and print encoding as input forms and, in principle, direct print input from compositors' tapes or similar. Braille and print encoding can be made either on- or off-line to the fairly large central computer configuration. There are direct Braille printers and Braille correcting terminals (shown on-line to the computer) for producing proof-reader's copy and for correcting the encoded Braille respectively. Output is achieved either via the direct Braille printers, for small numbers of copies, or via automatic stereotypes, for large numbers of copies. Automated or semi-automated post-embossing equipment is appropriate for this system.

Size of production. Large-scale: capacity dependent on number of encoding units, printers, correcting terminals, etc.; these in turn determined by capacity of central computer, especially if most are on-line.

Type of production. All types: Braille encoders can be used for more specialized material, print encoders for straightforward running prose.

Costs. High initial investment and large staff required for Braille and print encoding; also, many non-production personnel, e.g. computer specialists, required to run system. Thus, high labour costs.

Technical infrastructure. This must be at a high level, especially as any breakdown in the computer would cause practically the whole system to break down. Fast and effective service personnel must therefore be available.

Translation programme. Obviously essential for this system. Computer personnel

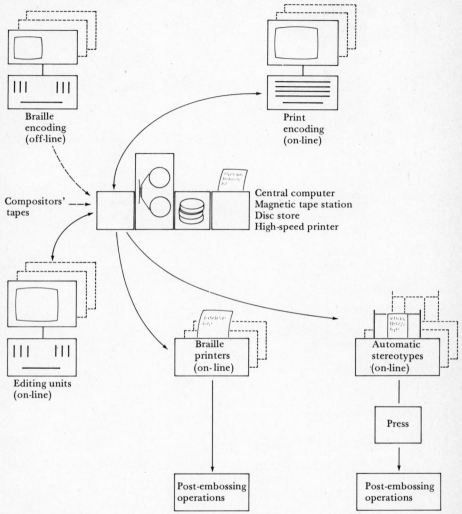

Fig. 5.   System I. Large-scale, computerized production system, largely on-line to central computer.

required for maintaining programmes and, if compositor tape input utilized, for writing conversion programmes for the different publishers' codes.

Existing resources. Such a system as this must entirely replace existing facilities. Investment costs are so high that the equipment must be used to the maximum if it is to be cost effective.

System II: Large-scale, microprocessor-bassed, computerized production system (see Fig. 6)

This system is built up from independent units, each capable of sophisticated

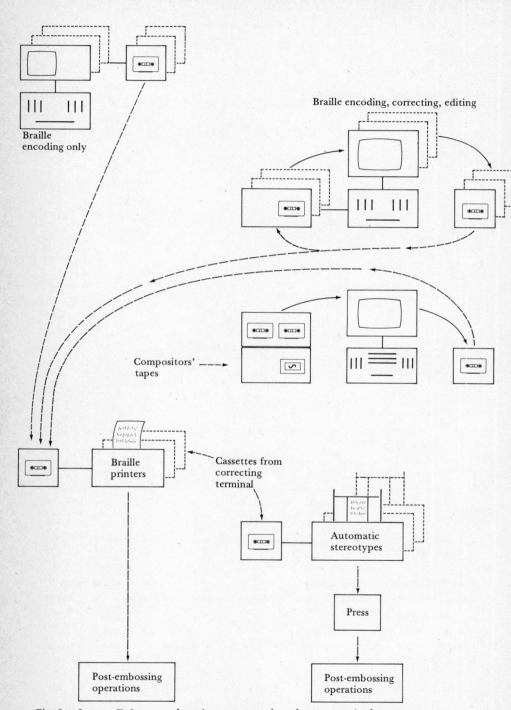

Braille encoding only

Braille encoding, correcting, editing

Compositors' tapes

Braille printers

Cassettes from correcting terminal

Automatic stereotypes

Press

Post-embossing operations

Post-embossing operations

Fig. 6.   System II. Large-scale, microprocessor-based, computerized system.

functions, thanks to the microprocessor-based technology. Figure 6 shows a configuration of Braille encoding units, Braille correcting/editing units (i.e. encoding units with an extra cassette reader for reading in encoded Braille text), and a Braille translation unit (i.e. a correcting/editing unit with extra processor capacity, another cassette reader for reading in various programmes, such as conversion programme for the different publishers' codes, Braille translation programmes, etc., and a paper-tape reader for reading in compositors' tapes or similar). The exact configuration of such a system can be adjusted to production needs. This can be achieved relatively easily as each unit is quite independent of any other, so the system can be built up gradually, if necessary. Braille printers provide proof-reading copy and small-scale output and automatic stereotypes are used for larger scale output. Automated or semi-automated post-embossing equipment is appropriate for this system.

Size of production. Large- to medium-scale production. Each machine is independent, therefore flexible in this respect.

Type of production. All types—Braille encoding for study material or similar, magazines, books. General book production supplemented by compositors' tape input.

Costs. High initial investment. However, such equipment can be used by existing transcribers, thus keeping increases in personnel costs to a minimum. Computer/ technical support required.

Technical infrastructure. This must be at a high level and a good supply of compositors' tapes should be available so as to avoid the necessity of having typists type in print text for translation. One advantage with regard to maintenance is that, as each unit is independent, breakdown in one machine does not have very important consequences for the functioning of the total system.

Translation programme. Programme obviously required for compositor tape input. As microprocessors are used, this programme would probably need to be developed specially for the system, although this situation could change in the near future.

Existing resources. Such a system can replace an existing system already having Braille transcribers. If appropriate, it can be introduced gradually; encoding and encoding/ editing units can gradually replace mechanical Braillewriters and stereotypes and output facilities increased in accordance. Production is most efficient, however, as a unified system.

System III: Medium-scale, computerized production system (see Fig. 7)

This system represents a situation where a computerized translation system has been introduced into an existing mechanical production system. The configuration shown in Figure 7 shows mechanical Braillewritter production continuing, with vacuum-form copying, for specialized material required in few copies. Manual stereotype

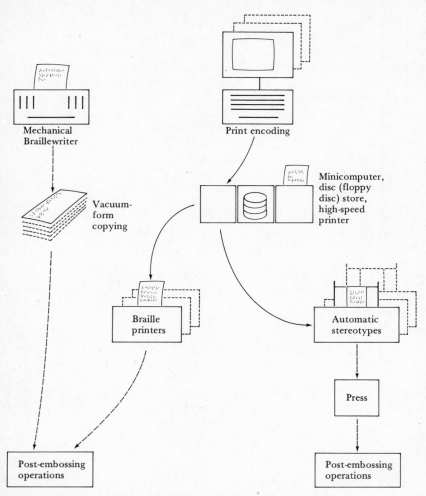

Mechanical Braillewriter

Print encoding

Vacuum-form copying

Minicomputer, disc (floppy disc) store, high-speed printer

Braille printers

Automatic stereotypes

Press

Post-embossing operations

Post-embossing operations

Fig. 7. System III. Medium-scale, computerized production system.

production has been replaced by print encoding to a minicomputer for automatic translation to Braille. Output is mainly via automatic stereotype, although a Braille printer can also exist for material required in fewer copies. Automated or semi-automated post-embossing equipment can be appropriate for this system.

Size of production. Large to medium—depending on capacity of computer.

Type of production. Predominant production is material in relatively large numbers of copies, often with tight time schedule.

Costs. Medium level of investment. New staff must be employed for print encoding, although a commercial bureau could be used.

Technical infrastructure. Such a system can be bought complete and service handled by an employee. Thus, demand for a generally high level technical infrastructure in the society is not so high as for the first two systems.

Translation programme. If in one of the main language areas, the translation programme could probably be bought as a package. Otherwise one must be developed.

Existing resources. This system could be introduced as a first stage of a more inclusive computerized system, or as a supplement to existing production facilities, which could continue in parallel. Advantage of computerization is to increase speed of production of magazine-type material, which previously was produced via manual stereotypes.

System IV: De-centralized Braille production system (Fig. 8)

This system consists of de-centralized Braille encoding equipment which allows small-scale Braille production and copying. Encoding and correction of the Braille is carried out on punched paper tape. For material required in a larger number of copies, the paper tape can be sent to a regional or central production centre (the latter could be either of the first two systems described above). This could be achieved either by actually sending the paper tapes by post or by transmitting the information encoded via the telephone network.

Size of production. Small-scale, but with access to larger-scale production by sending encoded tapes to a regional or central production centre having automated stereotypes.

Type of production. Local or individual needs mainly.

Costs. Low to medium investment. Decentralized transcribing units could be generally available so specially employed transcribers need not always be required. Running costs also dependent on relationship of decentralized units to regional or central facility.

Technical infrastructure. No special demands made in this respect. Decentralized units can be serviced by technician from regional or central facility.

Translation programme. Not required.

Existing recources. Such a decentralized organization could function in conjunction with a centralized facility such as described under Systems I and II. It could fulfil local and individual needs and function as a transcribing service. On the other hand, such Braille production organization can be appropriate for large countries having widely separated, perhaps both geographically and culturally, areas of population. These may well use different languages and almost certainly have localized requirements with respect to information and news, thus making any centralized facility difficult to

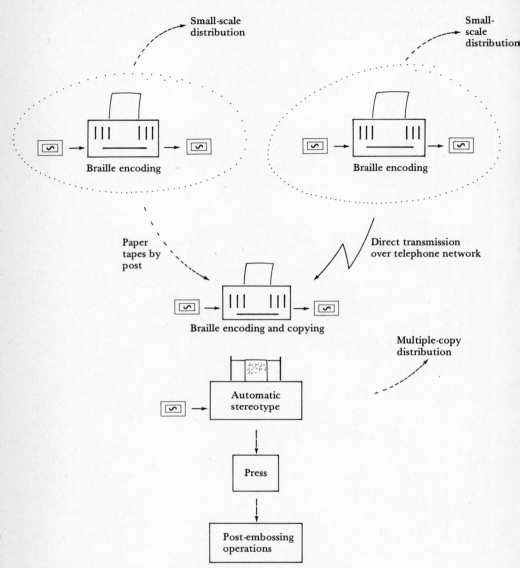

Fig. 8.   System IV. Decentralized Braille production system.

function efficiently. The system could function around a few regional centres which had automated stereotyping facilities, and post-embossing equipment. The largest part of transcribing can, however, take place at a local level.

System V: Mechanical Braille production system (see Fig. 9)

This production system was the 'standard' up until the 1960s (apart from the vacuum-form copying). It consists of two separate production techniques, operating in

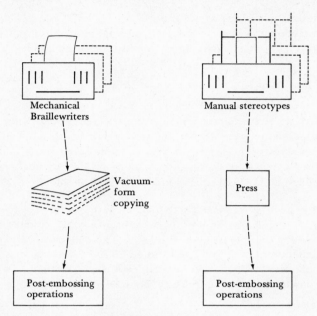

Fig. 9.   System V. Mechanical Braille production system.

parallel. Mechanical Braillewriters with vacuum-form copying used to produce materials in small numbers of copies. Stereotypes are used for larger-scale production.

Size of production. Small to large, depending on number of machines.

Type of production. All types.

Costs. Low to medium investment costs. Running costs can be relatively high owing to the expense of metal plates and plastic.

Technical infrastructure. No special demand for high level technical expertise.

Translation programme. Not required.

Existing resources. This system represents the most basic level of a Braille production facility.

Special production needs

Visually handicapped people are often at a special disadvantage in certain work situations which involve the handling of written information. There are, however, a number of technical aids which have been specifically developed to help the Braille user function independently in such work situations. Equipment relevant for two such areas of employment—secretarial and computer programmers—are discussed below.

Secretarial work

The equipment described in this section has, in fact, a considerably wider application than merely to people employed as secretaries. It extends to employment in any occupation which involves the writing of reports, memos, articles, etc., in print. Such activities are often carried out by academics, journalists, social workers, etc., all of which are possible employment areas for severely visually handicapped people.

Braille shorthand, stenography machines. These machines are specially designed for taking down letters and reports from dictation. They consist of a six-key Braille keyboard; the characters are embossed on to a roll of paper tape. These machines are compact and portable. Such equipment can be bought from: RNIB, United Kingdom (see Appendix B 1); Deutsche Blindenstudienanstalt, Federal Republic of Germany (see Appendix B 1); and Büromaschinen-Export GmbH, German Democratic Republic (see Appendix B 4).

Simultaneous inkprint/Braille typewriters. These are usually adaptations which can be fitted to ordinary electric typewriters and which allow the characters written on the typewriter to be simultaneously produced in Braille. Three such machines are listed in the *International Guide to Aids and Appliances* (see also Appendix B 4): El-Op Brailler, Israel; SP 200 Inkprint/Braille Typewriter, United States; Thiel Braillomat, Federal Republic of Germany. In addition, there is also a specially designed typewriter which can write both Braille and print characters, produced by Fuji Seisakusho Limited, Japan (see Appendix B 4).

Braille world-processing equipment. These are rather more sophisticated aids based on 'paperless' Braille equipment with word-processing capabilities (see Appendix E). These machines can be coupled to an ordinary electric typewriter, via a suitable interface. One such aid especially developed for this application is the BD-80 (Federal Republic of Germany) which is described in Appendix E.

Computer programming

Employment as a computer programmer or other work involving use of a computer has become a significant area of employment for visually handicapped persons in a number of countries. There is a considerable range of equipment which can be connected to a computer which allows the output to be directly available to a visually handicapped operator. These include a range of audio outputs as well as Braille; the latter only, however, will be described here.

Braille computer terminals can be categorized into three main groups according to their output forms: embossed tape, embossed pages, and mechanical Braille display.

Embossed tape. Three such machines are in current use, namely the Triformation BD-3 and ISE-1 (see Appendix B 3(b)), and the Thiel GmbH 'Braillomat' (see Appendix B 3(f)). The Triformation BD-3 was probably the first terminal for the visually handicapped to come on to the market and is one of the cheapest terminals available. The ISE-1, also from Triformation, represents a development of the BD-3 which allows better facilities for interactive use—it has its own keyboard and can be used remotely via a direct, acoustic, telephone link. The Thiel device is based on the 'Braillomat' equipment that has been available for some years. It consists basically of a device for writing Braille onto paper tape and which can be connected to a number of devices such as electric typewriters, telex, telephone, and computers. In the latter case, the equipment can be modified so that eight-dot Braille can be embossed on the tape, and also written from a Braille keyboard.

Embossed page. This group of devices has the greatest diversity of equipment which reflects the impetus the development of computer translation of Braille has given to the manufacture of direct Braille printers. Triformation (see Appendix B 3(b)) offers a range of page-embossing devices which can be connected to a computer. The LED-15, LED-30 and the LED-120 allow a maximum printout rate of 15, 30 and 120 characters per second respectively. Available options include a built-in acoustic coupler which gives the devices on-line capabilities for data processing. The standard typewriter keyboard can also be equipped with a switch which allows six keys to function in the same way as the keys on a Perkins brailler. All these devices allow the operator to read the last embossed line of characters without having to roll up the paper; the printout can be read as it is embossed.

SAGEM (see Appendix B 3(c)) offer two models—REM 8BR and TEM 8BR. The former is a receive-only unit, i.e. no keyboard, whereas the latter is provided with a built-in keyboard. An option is available so as to allow six keys on this keyboard to function in the same way as a Perkins brailler. Both models can be bought with a punched paper-tape reader and the TEM model with a paper tape punch. Also, a Braille telex converter is available. Maximum print-out rate of both models is fifteen characters per second.

A different kind of device is that developed by Loeber at IBM in California. This allows 'either inkprint Braille [to be] produced with an IBM Magnetic Card SELECTRIC typewriter equipped with a read only translation chip and an embosser. Embossing is done on the front side of the paper so the operator can read the information as it is embossed.'[37] This is achieved by substituting an electromechanical device for the typewriter platen, which contains a stylus assembly operated by six solenoids. Also, a special type-ball with dot depressions corresponding to a single Braille cell pattern is substituted for the standard type-ball. Embossing a Braille character 'is accomplished by operating the solenoids, projecting the desired dots forward and then impacting the type-ball with its dot depressions against the protruding pins',[38] thus forming dots on the front of the paper.

In addition to these special devices, modifications can be made to existing line printers so that they produce Braille instead of print. One such commercially available modification is a fairly straightforward replacement of a single part of the printing mechanism on an IBM 1403 printer, although some adjustment of the printer will be necessary to achieve the best possible quality of embossing which will require an experienced technician to carry out.

Mechanical Braille displays. Some of the available mechanical Braille display equipment can be connected to a computer, allowing their use as an ordinary terminal. The display length of many of them, however, limits their usefulness in the particular application. Two devices—Brailink (Clark & Smith, United Kingdom) and Schönherr's equipment—have been specially designed for application with computers. (These are described in Appendix E.)

Notes

1. B. Hampshire and T. Whiston, 'On the Manual Transcription of Braille', *Applied Ergonomics,* Vol. 8, No. 3, 1977, p. 159–63.
2. Personal communication, 29 November 1978, from Harry J. Friedman, Manager, Howe Press of Perkins School for the Blind, Watertown, Mass. (United States).
3. American Foundation for the Blind (AFB), *International Guide to Aids and Appliances for Blind and Visually Handicapped Persons,* p. 3, New York, N.Y., 1977.
4. Personal communication, 9 November 1978, from Professor K. O. Beatty, North Carolina State University (United States).
5. Personal communication, 2 November 1978, from Howard Bellamy, Technical Director, Micronex Limited.
6. Keyboards currently used by Braille transcribers are 'chord' keyboards. That is, combinations ('chords') of the six keys can be pressed, thus allowing all 63 Braille characters to be generated from the six keys.
7. R. Seibel, 'Data Entry Devices and Procedures', in Van Cott and Kinkade (eds.), *Human Engineering Guide to Equipment Design,* rev. ed., p. 319, Washington, D.C., U.S. Government Printing Office, 1972.
8. J. W. Schoonard and S. J. Boies, 'Short-Type: A Behavioural Analysis of Typing and Text Entry', *Human Factors,* Vol. 17, No. 2, 1975, p. 203–14.
9. N. C. Loeber, 'Using Punched Cards for Automated Braille Embossing' (n.d.). (Available from Dr Loeber, IBM Corporation, 5600 Cottle Road, San Jose, Calif. 95193 (United States).)
10. Ibid., p. 1.
11. Braille Printing Techniques. Rational printing procedures for Braille Grade 2 and tactile graphics. Six reports have been published from this project by Stiftung Rehabilitation, Postfach 101409, 6900 Heidelberg 1 (Federal Republic of Germany): H. J. Küppers, *Abschlussbericht (Übersicht) / Final Report (An Overview)* (Ord. No. S.1098; Ord. No. S.1115 English edition); C. Brösamle and U. Lehman, *Texterfassung für den Blindenbuchdruck mit Schreibautomation* [Text-Editing for Braille Book Printing with Text-Editing Machines] (Ord. No. S.1099); C. Brösamle and U. Lehman, *Braille-Bücher aus Druckerei-Datenträgern* [Braille Books from Compositors' Tape Data Carriers] (Ord. No. S.1105); M. Harres, *Textautomat für Blindenschrift* [Text-Editing Machine for Braille] (Ord. No. S.1100); S. D. Glitsch and E. Riefer, *Datenträgergesteuerte Punziermaschine* [Data-Controlled Stereotyper] (Ord. No. S.1101); H. J. Küppers, *Neue Verfahren zur Reproduktion bildlicher Darstellungen in taktiler Form für den Blindenbuchdruck* [New Procedures for the Reproduction of Graphics in Tactile Form for Braille Book Printing] (Ord. No. S.1102). (The last five publications are available in German only.)
12. These tactile modules were developed by and are available from: K. P. Schonherr, Schloss Solitude, Geb 3, D-7000, Stuttgart 1 (Federal Republic of Germany).
13. Brösamle and Lehman, op. cit.
14. C. Brösamle, 'Braille Books from Compositors' Tapes', *Braille Research Newsletter,* No. 5, July 1977, p. 13-18.

15. A special correcting slate, consisting of four lines, each of 40 characters, is available from the Royal National Institute for the Blind, London (Cat. No. 9028). This enables correction to be made on a sheet of Braille produced on a Perkins brailler after proof-reading. A plastic eraser stylus is available from RNIB (Cat. No. 9487).

16. Schonherr, op. cit.

17. J. E. Sullivan, 'Braille Systems', *Braille Research Newsletter*, No. 5, July 1977, p. 35–49.

18. D. A. G. Brown, 'The Introduction of Braille Produced by Computer at the Canadian National Institute for the Blind', *Braille Research Newsletter*, No. 6, October 1977, p. 6.

19. Dr H. J. Küppers, Stiftung Rehabilitation, Postfach 101409, 6900 Heidelberg 1 (Federal Republic of Germany).

20. Herbert Jakob, Deütsche Zentralbücherei für Blinde zu Leipzig, 701 Leipzig, Gustav-Adolf Str. 7 (German Democratic Republic).

21. Personal communication, 27 October 1978, from Anton Hastig, manager of the Braille Printing House and Library of Austria.

22. Personal communication, 8 November 1978, from Monique Truquet, Centre TOBIA.

23. P. A. Fortier, D. Keeping and D. R. Young, 'Braille: A Bilingual (French/English) System for Computer-Aided Braille Translation', *Braille Research Newsletter*, No. 7, March 1978, p. 36.

24. P. W. F. Coleman, 'Some Thoughts on PC/1 Braille Translators', *Braille Automation Newsletter*, December 1976, p. 8–15.

25. W. A. Slaby, 'The Marker System of Production Rules—A Universal Braille Translator', in R. A. J. Gildea, G. Hubner and H. Wessner (eds.), *Computerised Braille Production; Proceedings of the First International Workshop in Münster (Federal Republic of Germany), March 1973*, Rechenzentrum den Universität Münster, 1974. (Reprinted as 'Proceedings of the Workshop Towards the Communality of Algorithms Among Braille Transcription Systems for Multi-lingual Usage, University of Münster, Federal Republic of Germany, March 1973', *SIGCAPH Newsletter*, No. 15, March 1975.)

26. In addition, research is being carried out in a number of universities and other research institutes. More detailed information can be obtained from the World Council for the Welfare of the Blind (WCWB) Sub-Committee on Computerised Braille Production (see Appendix B 3(c)).

27. Personal communication, 9 October 1978, from Derrick Croisdale, Chairman, WCWB Sub-Committee on Computerised Braille Production and other Media.

28. J. M. Gill, 'Available Page Braille Embossers', *Braille Automation Newsletter*, December 1976, p. 16–29.

29. Personal communication, 23 October 1978, from Jenny Aulinger, IBM Europe, Paris.

30. H. J. Küppers, *Braille Printing Techniques—Final Report*, 1976 (Ord. No. S.1115).

31. *PED 30. A New Era in Braille Book Production.* Manufacturer's brochure, Triformation Systems Inc.

32. Dr A. N. L. Westland, 'The Design of a Fast Braille Lineprinter', *Braille Automation Newsletter*, December 1976, p. 3–7.

33. A 'burster' is the name given to equipment which separates perforated fan-folded stationery in single sheets. Equipment can also be bought which can trim the paper down to a specific size as part of the separating process.

34. 'Collator' is the name generally adopted by the machine manufacturer to describe equipment which, by semi-automatic or fully automatic means, enable single leaves or folded sections to be assembled upon each other to form a set or a book. But from the printer's and bookbinder's point of view, this operation is known as 'gathering'. Machines performing this operation will be referred to as collators in this book.

35. Reply, from the manager of the Scottish Braille Press, to questionnaire sent out in February 1977 by B. Hampshire.

36. Reply, from Howe Press of Perkins School for the Blind, to questionnaire sent out in February 1977 by B. Hampshire.

37. N. C. Loeber, *Modifications to the IBM Magnetic Card Selectric Typewriter and 2741 Communication Terminal for Braille Translation and Embossing*, p. 1 (IBM 37.303/January 1976, Technical Report).

38. Ibid., p. 11.

Chapter 4

Braille code systems

Introduction and historical background

The most important landmark in the development of Braille code systems in recent times was the publication, by Unesco in 1954, of Sir Clutha Mackenzie's *World Braille Usage*. The production of this work established the general, although not exclusive, agreement about the principle of 'same sound—same sign', using the 1878 allocation of signs as the basis. This publication, together with the establishment of the World Braille Council (WBC) in 1952, was the culmination of Unesco's support for Braille which began in 1949.

The function of WBC was 'to act in an advisory capacity on the interpretation and application of Braille principles, to coordinate future Braille developments, to advise on such Braille problems as might be referred to it from time to time and to act as a centre for the collation and exchange of information on Braille.'[1] Among the problems defined by WBC at the time of its creation, the solution of which should be their focus of activity, were the following:

unification of music notation
unification of scientific and mathematical notation
establishment of a general catalogue of Braille publications
creation of regional committees for the development of a sound system of abbreviations applicable to the language of each region
application of Braille to tribal languages.[2]

Activities around the development of a world music notation, Spanish (and Portuguese) contracted Braille, and uniformity of mathematical and scientific symbols, dominated WBC work for the five years after the 1954 WCWB World Assembly.

World music notation

Regarding world music notation, a conference was organized in 1954, under the sponsorship of Unesco, WCWB and WBC, to consider the improvement and extension of uniformity in the field of Braille music notation. As a result of this conference, H. V. Spanner was assigned the task of translating its decisions into an acceptable Revised Manual. Mackenzie describes the subsequent events as follows:

Mr Spanner ... referred his proposals to all the countries concerned for acceptance or comment, and finally submitted his whole work to a special committee consisting of Dr Rodenberg, Prof. Dr Reuss and Mr Sinclair Logan for final voting. On their approving the draft, the Manual was printed. (Revised International Manual of Braille Music Notation—1956—Part I Western Music). Subsequently, however, Dr Reuss raised a number of queries and placed proposals for the inclusion of additional notation. His early proposals we (WBC) agreed to accept but on his countering with further requirements we replied that these must necessarily be held over for a subsequent world meeting. He then withdrew his permission for the inclusion of the earlier material.[3]

In 1960 Dr Reuss presented his code system which took into account the symbols adopted by the International Congress of Braille Music Notation held in Paris in 1929. This resulted in a division among blind musicians; English-speaking countries defending the Spanner Method while France, the Federal Republic of Germany, and the USSR among others supported Dr Reuss's proposals.

This division still exists with somewhat differing accounts of the course of events after 1960. At the present time, national considerations dominate the international ones, and any significant change seems unlikely in the near future.

World mathematics notation

During the 1959 WCWB World Assembly, thoughts concerning the possibility of achieving any unification of mathematical notation were pessimistic. The main reasons for this pessimism were: the major producers of Braille have their own system to which they adhere; new symbols in inkprint are appearing all the time, which vary between countries and authors; and blind persons rarely borrow books on higher mathematics from foreign countries.[4]

It was suggested, however, that unification was desirable up to a certain level of mathematical knowledge (i.e. the kind of equations and calculations one might expect in a popular article). As regards more advanced mathematics, agreement should be sought on general principles rather than on a comprehensive system. There was, however, some disagreement on this point.

A system developed in Japan, taking the Taylor system as a basis, was considered a possibility for a world code during the early 1960s. Nothing concrete happened, however, with regard to the adoption of this system for world usage.

In 1963 the Soviet Association of the Blind decided to develop a unified system of Braille scientific notation taking the 1929 Marburg system as their starting point. Its new system was completed in 1973 and an English translation was published in 1975. Following this, the Soviet Association sponsored, in 1976, an international meeting on the 'unification of Braille mathematics and science notation'. Twelve countries were represented and representatives from France, the Federal Republic of Germany, the

Netherlands, Poland, Spain, USSR, the United Kingdon and the United States presented papers on the code systems in use.

At approximately the same time, another notation was being developed in Spain.[5] This is known as the 'U' notation and is also based on the common signs of the Marburg system.

The international role of the Soviet and Spanish systems appears to be somewhat unclear at the present time. A number of countries have adopted one or other of these codes so that a division seems a likely outcome.

In the United States a completely new code has been developed known as the Nemeth Code.[6] This is a completely original development which uses quite different principles to the European codes.

Literary Braille codes

The impetus given to work on literary Braille codes by *World Braille Usage* and the 1954 WCWB World Assembly continued through to the 1964 WCWB Assembly. This was the last assembly where Sir Clutha Mackenzie was chairman of the WBC, and his summary of the work of the WBC during the previous fifteen years is worth reproducing.

The following languages have been furnished with new and uniform Braille systems:

European Languages: In consultation with the Braille authorities in Yugoslavia we worked out Braille systems for Serbo-Croat, Slovene, Macedonian and Albanian. For many years in consultation with the authorities in Spain, Portugal and Latin America, the Council worked steadily towards bringing about uniformity as between Spain and Portugal in Europe and the countries of Latin America. This at last appears to have reached a final satisfactory result.

Arabic: A single Arabic Braille was provided for the whole Arabic area throughout Asia and Africa to replace about a dozen conflicting systems.

Asia: For the Braille systems of Turkey, Armenia, Persia, Pakistan (Urdu), the main languages of India (Devanagari, Bengali, Uriah, Tamil, Malayalam, Gujarati, Kanarese Sikh), Ceylon[7] (Sinhalese), Malay, Indonesia (Bahasa), Taiwan (Taiwanese), and the Philippines (Tagalog), satisfactory uniform Braille systems have been brought into existence. On a mission to China in 1947 I made recommendations regarding a single Chinese Braille to replace its seven or eight earlier existing systems. One of these, Cantonese, had retained the original Braille signs for the Roman alphabet plus many additional signs and tone mark and we suggested that in principle this system should be followed throughout the country. . . .

Africa: In addition to the Arabic of North Africa, revised Braille systems have been provided for Hausa, Dogon, Amharic (Ethiopia), Twi, Ibo, and Nyanja of West Africa, and Shona of Southern Rhodesia. Dr Walter Cohen, who is a member of the World Braille Council has provided modern Braille systems for three South African native languages, namely Zulu-Xhosa, Northern Sotho, and Southern Sotho.

Pacific: At the request of Samoa, the World Braille Council approved a Braille system for this language and this in turn has been passed on to American Samoa.[8]

The work on new Braille codes continued, but this area of Braille gradually assumed a less prominent place in international meetings. This may have been, in part, due to the increasing dominance of technological developments in discussions around Braille during this time. Technological developments have also had, however, a certain influence on Braille codes, resulting from the development of computer programmes to translate inkprint to Braille [9] and the use of computers in language analysis for the study of some aspects of the efficiency of Braille code systems. [10]

Such influences have led to at least two code systems being 'rationalized'—German and Danish—and, currently, there is a project under way to study the possible rationalization of the English Braille code. [11]

Literary Braille codes

Problems in developing code for a language not having one

by Walter Cohen, M.A., Ph.D.

While knowledge of the principles of the Braille system is essential to those having to develop a Braille code—specifically for a language which does not possess such a Braille code—a detailed knowledge of the language in question, though desirable, is not always a prerequisite. This I discovered during the ten year period when I was Chairman for the former World Braille Council and in this capacity received requests for Braille codes for various languages, some of which I had never heard of before.

The position often arises that blind people, familiar with one Braille system, are impatient of an uncontracted system for a new language and take no account of the difficulties of those facing the challenge of translating those elusive little dots into something intelligible. The watchword in devising a new Braille code is 'make haste slowly' in introducing contractions and abbreviations.

Most countries requiring a new Braille code will face the example of an existing code, e.g. an Indian language in Ecuador would have to take Spanish Braille into account, an African language may have experienced the impact of English or French. Confusion between the new Braille code and that of the official language of the country has to be avoided, as I endeavoured to do in the case of the Ecuador Indians.

Frequently, missionaries from various denominations establish some form of care for the blind in the country in which they are working and in their fervour to bring the Gospel to new converts, they tend to give the scriptures and other religious material priority in devising a local Braille code. Many words are thus contracted because of the frequency of their appearance in religious literature but are found to be redundant when the reader turns to recreational and study material in Braille. Competing Braille codes have been found to exist within a single country in Asia, because they were devised by missionaries of various denominations. It is not always the easiest task to find a compromise code acceptable to all.

The literature

It is often found that those countries without a Braille code also have a somewhat embryonic literature. In such cases, there is not a great variety of literature on which to work to determine the minimal requirements of a new Braille code. He who devises the code may find, as I did, that when blind readers settle down to a careful study of such a code, they complain that certain Braille symbols, while correct in terms of Braille principles, do not 'feel' right to the fingertips. Invariably they were proved right.

Some languages on which I have been privileged to work have only seven letters in the alphabet and one is tempted to use the remaining nine basic Braille symbols for contraction, etc., but then I found that English Braille had already been taught to the readers, so that confusion between the new and the old established code must be avoided, especially in the case of children.

The temptation to use phonetics must be avoided at all costs because spelling and writing will suffer if anyone treads this dangerous ground.

Finally, language is a living thing and, as a language develops, so must its Braille code. The code should come up for constant review so as to include new words, new concepts and be flexible.

Demands for more and more contractions and abbreviations as the literature of the language in question develops must be approached with caution, because while there are the impatient intelligentsia, there are also, and perhaps even more important, the new pupils struggling to master the system which is based on only six dots but which opens up words and worlds for the blind everywhere.

Characteristics of Braille code systems

The available character set for Braille amounts to just sixty-three characters compared to the, in principle, limitless character set for print symbols. The implication of this, in practice, is that new symbols can be simply created when needed for print whereas in Braille new 'characters' can only be created by combining characters from the existing set.

This, together with the size and spacing necessary for Braille cells, means that transcription from print to Braille involves a significant increase in the bulk of Braille books compared to their print originals. This, among other factors, has resulted in many languages using contracted Braille codes. However, since the Braille character set is limited, many of the Braille characters must take on multiple meanings. This, in turn, means that a set of rules must be developed so that the different meanings of a Braille character can be determined and that their use does not interfere with the reading process generally.

There are, then, two main aspects to be considered in any analysis of a Braille code: the 'efficiency' of the contractions used and the rules of use of contractions.

Efficiency of contractions

Space saving. There have been a number of studies examining the efficiency of contractions with regard to how much space they save.[12] In general, contraction systems emerge rather badly in this aspect of efficiency.

The Kederis et al. study[13] was based on the print equivalent of 291,000 words, which is equivalent of nearly a million Braille characters. The sample ranged from children at grade 3 level to adults, and from verses and rhymes to history texts. Account was taken of the fact that the occurrence of some elements would be different in Braille and in print, because of the rules of Braille usage. For example, if the EA and ED letter sequences were being counted in print, their occurrence in the words 'uneasy' and 'reduce' would add to their total. They would not be counted, however, in Braille, as their use would violate the rules of the American code.

In their paper, they give full tables of their results. These can be summarized by saying that grade 2 Braille saves 31 per cent of letter-spaces over inkprint, and that Braille used 26.5 per cent fewer characters.

The range of occurrence of the Braille characters was from 61,862 for the letter 'E' to zero for the ampersand, fraction line, per cent sign, and the words 'Braille', 'conceiving', 'declaring' and 'deceiving'. Only 76 out of the 255 symbols that are represented by one or two cell Braille characters occurred over 1,000 times, and of the Braille contractions included within these 76 Braille characters, they saved 75 per cent of the total letter-spaces saved by all contractions.

Gill and Humphreys report an analysis of frequency of use of Braille contractions.[14] The data used consisted of slightly over 1 million words which were obtained from the material translated by the short document service at the Warwick Research Unit for the Blind. Their results showed the following:

The use of a system of contractions saved 1,257,640 Braille cells for the test data of 1,073,339 words. The first 13 contractions account for over 50% of the space saving, and the first 36 contractions for over 75 per cent. The last 11 contractions occur, in total, only 38 times in over one million words.

The contractions AND, FOR, WITH, THE account for 23 per cent of the space saving but all the 23 simple upper word-signs together only account for 8.2 per cent.

Gill[15] has continued this work using two data bases, one of 2.3 million words of English text and one of 1 million words of American English which is the Brown Corpus. Programmes have been developed to count

(i) the frequency of use of contractions in the present contracted Braille code (English version) and in modified codes needed as part of the joint Warwick/Birmingham project [see Chapter 7]
(ii) the frequency of use of words
(iii) the frequency of groups of letters at the beginning, in the middle and at the end of words.

Reading speed.   The influence of the Braille code on reading has been discussed in Chapter 6. From research, two conflicting factors emerge which must be balanced if reading speed, and reading ease, are to be optimized.

On the one hand, by reducing the number of characters in the text through the use of contractions, reading speed is enhanced by reducing the number of characters to be perceived, and increasing the amount of 'information' in a proportion of the perceptual units, i.e. Braille characters.

On the other hand, by reducing the number of characters in the text through the use of contractions, the reading process can be hindered by the reduction in the redundancy in the text (see page 116) and by increasing the 'cognitive load' on the reader through increasing the amount of 'decoding' required by contracted text.

Rules of use of contractions

In *World Braille Usage,* Mackenzie offered some guiding considerations for the design of contracted Braille systems which are worth repeating.

The secrets of a good contracted system seem to be:
(a) The greatest possible use being made of the mnemonic principle;
(b) Each sign to have as few meanings as possible;
(c) The rules, governing the use of contractions, to be few and clear;
(d) The text not to be so transmuted that little remains of the context to hint to the reader the basic form of the word. The main stem of all but the commonest words should retain some semblance of their original selves; and
(e) The system to be such that without undue mental effort children can learn it by the end of their primary education and newly blind adults in from two to four months. From the end of the primary stage with children this is important because their education is greatly stimulated if they have ready access to general literature.

These 'guiding principles' fit in rather well with the findings of research studies regarding learning and reading Braille discussed in Chapter 6.

The development of computer-aided translation, however, has bought a new dimension to the question of rules of use of contractions. When Braille translation programmes were first being developed, many computer programmers felt, and some still do, great frustration at the fact that the Braille systems used rules related to such language-related features as syllables, sentence structure, pronounciation, etc., which are not all easy to define for a translation programme.

A workshop was held in 1976 to specifically discuss the contraction system of American English Braille in the context of computer-aided production.[16] The report contains many 'position papers' from experts on the question of Braille contractions and their rules of usage. These opinions differ widely: for example compare the following two statements:

There are many cases where using a contraction regardless of syllabification of pronounciation would be devasting to the readability of a word. Consider the following examples and you will see. Suppose I were to permit the contraction for 'name' in the word 'ornament'. Suppose I were to permit the contraction for 'time' in the word 'sentiment'. . . . To allow contractions regardless of pronounciation or readability is a rash recommendation.[17] . . . good perceivers (be it of print, Braille, or Morse code) do not attend to the elements of the code, but attend to patterns. These patterns do not, in themselves, have meaning—semantic content; it is left up to the perceiver to impose meaning on them. For example, when reading 'care' in print or listening to 'care' in Morse, one does not infer the word 'car' a meaningful constituent. Unlike most other codes, Braille attempts to impose meaning on the constituents of patterns. For example, the contraction for the letter sequence 'n-a-m-e' can't be used in a larger pattern unless it sounds like the word 'name'. Contrary to popular opinion, this attempt to preserve semantic content of constituents of patterns decreases rather than enhances readability.[18]

The proceedings of this workshop give a good insight into just how complex this question of Braille contractions is, and also, into the extent which there is disagreement among the experts on many points.

Mathematical codes

The mathematical codes in current use may be categorized into four groups which relate, albeit rather loosely, to their original source.[19]

Group I: Code by H. M. Taylor. This is used in Japan, Brazil and Israel. Brazil, however, following an Ibero-american meeting in Buenos Aires in 1973, has accepted the Spanish 'U' notation. Taylor's code was first presented in 1917 and was adopted as the English standard at that time. The code used by Japan, although taking the Taylor system as a starting point, has developed it considerably. They have, for example, carried out statistical frequency studies to determine the optimal assignment of Braille characters to mathematical symbols. Their code, as a result, is very much more developed and sophisticated than the original Taylor system.

Group II: The French and the Portuguese codes. The main feature of these codes is the use of the following symbols for the numbers.

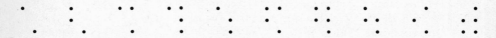

This is a restriction to the further development of symbols.

Group III: The Marburg system. This was presented first in 1929. Codes developed from this original include those used in the United Kingdom, the Federal Republic of Germany, the Netherlands, Italy, Sweden, Denmark, the Soviet Union, Argentina, Guatemala and Spain.

Group IV: The Nemeth code. This was an original development by Professor Nemeth of the University of Detroit. Its main feature is that it transcribes the signs through the representation of the component elements of the inkprint symbol. The Bharati Braille code for mathematics used in India is based on the Nemeth code. The Nemeth code is also used in the Philippines and Thailand.

In Appendix F the differences between the Nemeth code and the 'U' notation are described in some detail.

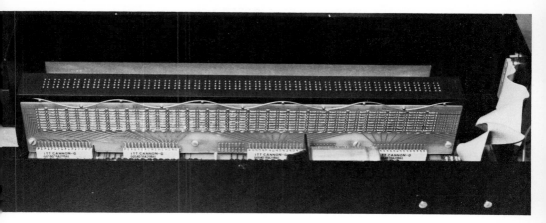

...ille display module consisting
...orty characters of eight dots each.
...e extra two dots are used for
...resenting special control
...racters.

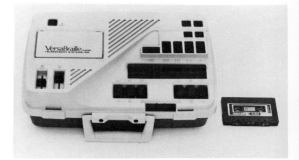

Versabraille. A paperless Braille
recorder produced by Telesensory
Systems Inc. (United States of
America).

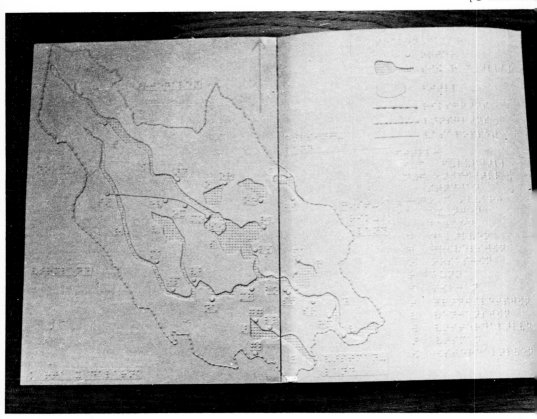

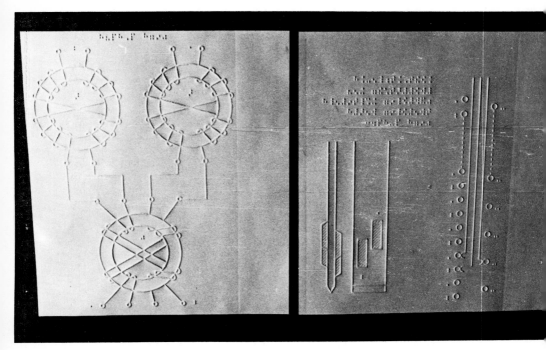

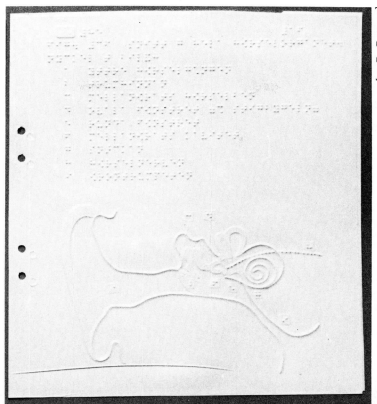

Some examples
of tactile maps
and diagrams.

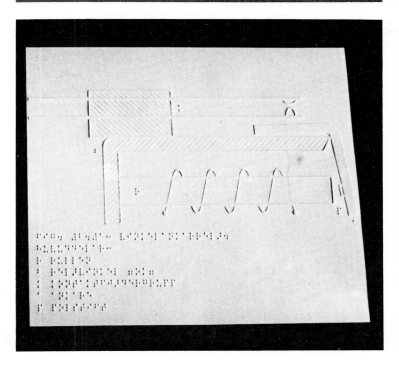

A slate and stylu

The Perkins
Braillewriter.

(a)

Large-scale computerized Braille production system. These pictures illustrate RNIB's computerized production system in London.

(a) Cassette-based encoding unit. The text from these off-line units are read into the computer system for correction.
(b) The central computer installation.
(c) On-line encoding terminals for direct input of text into the computer. There it is automatically converted to contracted Braille.
(d) One of four Braille editing machines connected on-line to the computer

(b)

(c)

(d)

Large-scale
microprocessor-based
system.
These pictures illustrate
the Swedish Federation
the Visually Handicappe
Braille production syste
in Stockholm.

(a) Cassette encoding u
with Braille display
connected so that a
visually handicapped
person can use the
equipment.

(b) Braille encoding/
editing unit. A Braille
display and a standard
keyboard can also be
connected to this unit.
[© Eric Blücher]

(c) Programmable unit f
conversion and editing
text from inkprint to
Braille.

Some examples of Braille output devices.
(a) SAGEM 8 REM Braille printer.
(b) Triformation's LED-120 Braille printer.
(c) Triformation's PED-30 plate embosser.

(a)

(b)

(c)

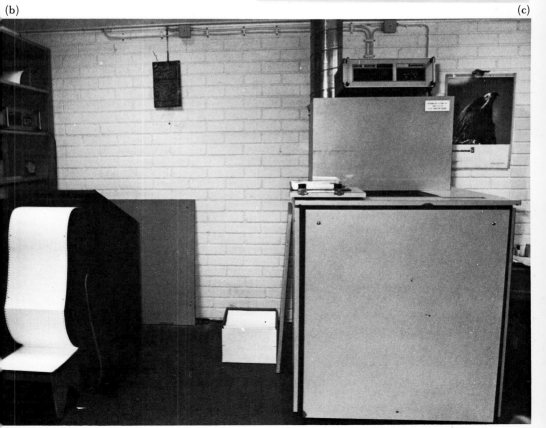

Heidelberg GTS automatic feed press. [© Bo Prägare.]

The inkprint book in the foreground became the thirteen Braille volumes shown behind.

Braille music codes

Braille music notation is based on the first ten Braille characters:

Alphabet	A	B	C	D	E	F	G	H	I	J

Quavers or 1/128ths	Rest	C	D	E	F	G	A	B

Crotchets or 1/64ths	Rest	C	D	E	F	G	A	B

Minims or 1/32nds	Rest	C	D	E	F	G	A	B

Semibreves or 1/16ths	Rest	C	D	E	F	G	A	B

Pitch is indicated by seven 'octave signs' which indicate the particular octave in which a note appears. These pitch signs are:

1st	2nd	3rd	4th	5th	6th	7th

Accidentals are formed by adding dot 6 to the alphabetical characters A, B and C, thus:

♮.   ♭:.   ♯:.

With regard to note-grouping, the general principle is to write the first note of the group in its true value and the remaining notes are then written in quavers.

When two or more notes of the same value are sounded together, forming a chord, one note only is written, the remainder being represented by signs which indicate their distance of interval from the written note. These interval signs are as follows:

Unison	2nd	3rd	4th	5th	6th	7th	Octave

Intervals are read downwards in the treble clef and upwards in the bass clef.

Braille music notation 'represents a condensation of a musical score to its lowest possible terms of statement. A good Braille transcript of an inkprint score will frequently reduce the actual notation to something approximating to a précis by means of special devices of contraction and abbreviation.'[20]

The international differences regarding Braille notations relate to the disposition of the score rather than the assignment of meanings to Braille characters. Spanner summarizes the situation with regard to score disposition well:

In all types of music, whether vocal or instrumental, the inkprint score is set out in such a manner that the eye can take in several staves together, or one stave at a time, or else a particular melodic or harmonic line by itself, as the reader wishes. In Braille, the fingers can only read one, at most two, signs at a time according to whether one or two hands are used. It is therefore of special concern to the blind reader (and to the transcriber whether seeing or blind) that a satisfactory plan be found for the arrangement of the music text on the Braille page.

The problem resolves itself into the alternatives of (i) following the music of one part at a time and (ii) attempting by means of short sections for each part—the measure being a convenient unit—to read one part alternately with another, memorising the first sufficiently to be able to combine it with the next, and so on. The difficulty is increased by the fact that when both hands are used for reading it is impossible to read and play at the same time.

The early history of Braille notation shows that the first of these alternatives was chosen as the most practical line of development, the result finally emerging as a score in which, for keyboard instruments, the music for the right hand was given first, followed by that for the left hand, and in organ music by that for the pedals. Occasionally (in vocal music invariably) the whole of a piece or movement was given thus in each part; more usually a number of measures chosen by the transcriber on musical grounds was made the unit of the paragraph.

At the beginning of the present century there was a gradual rise of feeling against the disposition of the score on the ground that it prevented the reader from obtaining an immediate and complete sound-picture of each measure, and so experiments were tried with the second alternative, which resulted in three distinct methods of presentation:
(1) the writing of the complete score at once (. . . 'Vertical Score' . . .);
(2) the writing of a measure of one hand followed by its counterpart in the other (. . . 'Bar by Bar'. . .);
(3) the placing of the parts in parallel lines as in ink-print.
Of these methods, the third has proved to be the most capable of development, branching out into the following forms:
(a) bar over bar;
(b) count over count;
(c) open score (in which each melodic line or 'voice' is given separately, bar over bar);
(d) line over line, a rough approximation to bar over bar.[21]

In Figure 1 a score is shown translated into both Bar over Bar and Bar by Bar dispositions.

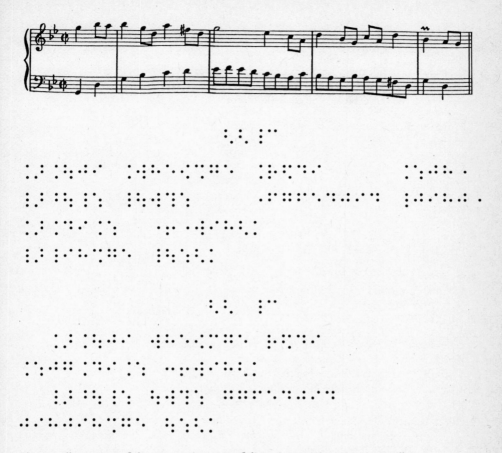

Fig. 1. Illustration of the two main ways of disposing music scores in Braille.

Computer Braille codes

A special code for computer use is necessary as, when writing a program, every letter, number or punctuation mark has significance. This means that ideally there should always be a one-to-one correspondence between inkprint and Braille symbols. This ideal is not possible to attain, however, as there are more than sixty-three characters that need to be represented.

The major difference between computer codes and the literary codes is the representation of numbers. The codes used in Europe add dot 6 to the letters 'a' to 'j' in order to represent numbers. In the United States (and other countries following the Nemeth mathematics code) the letters 'a' to 'j' are written as lower signs.

There are a number of different conventions concerning other symbols and some examples are given in Table 1.

Working with Braille

Table 1. Some common symbols represented in three different computer codes

Symbol	American	Dutch	Russian
Comma	6	2	2
Semi-colon	4,5	2,5	6 and 2,3 §
Full-stop	4,6	2,5,6	2,5,6
Question mark	1,4,6	2,6	6 and 2,6 §
Apostrophe	3	3	3,5,6
Quotation mark	5,6	3,5,6	6 and 2,3,6 (open) §
			6 and 2,5,6 (close) §
Plus	3,4,6	2,3,5	2,3,5
Equals	1,5,6	2,3,5,6	2,3,5,6
Less than	2,3,4,5,6	5,6	4 and 2,4,6 §
Greater than	1,2,3,4,5,6	4,5	4 and 1,3,5 §
Minus	3,6	3,6	6 and 3,6 §
Slash	3,4	3,4	6 and 3,4 §
Left bracket	1,2,6	2,3,6	1,2,6
Right bracket	3,4,5	3,4,5	3,4,5

§ means double-sign is used

Details of the various computer codes can be obtained from the following:
1. British   RNIB London (Appendix A)
2. Dutch   Dutch Library for the Blind (Appendix A)
3. German   Deutsche Blindenstudienanstalt (Appendix A)
4. French   Association Valentin Haüy (Appendix A)
5. Russian   All-Russia Association of the Blind,
        Novaja Plochad 14, Moscow, USSR
6. Spanish   ONCE (Appendix A)
7. American   Currently a project is being carried out to study computer code and to
        recommend necessary and proper revisions. Details from:
            Dr M. Hooper
            Visual Disabilities Braille Project
            101-C Education Building
            Education Building
            College of Education
            Tallahassee, Fla

Phonetic code

Within linguistic science, the International Phonetic Alphabet (IPA) is usually used. Certain languages or language areas have, however, developed special systems of their own. The IPA attempts to characterize each and every sound by a single character, although there are characters which modify in various ways these sound representations, through accent, tone, length, open or closed, etc.

This phonetic alphabet has been translated into Braille and a basic work is the British book, *A Braille Notation of the International Phonetic Alphabet.*[22] The more recent American work *A Code of Braille Textbook Formats and Techniques* builds in part on the earlier British work.[23] Differences do exist, however, with respect to phonetic notation, particularly with regard to phonetic brackets. The Braille phonetic code system will be discussed in detail in the new edition of *World Braille Usage.*

Diacritic symbols in Braille

by John Jarvis

The publishers of dictionaries and other similar reference books in which diacritic symbols are required differ widely in their choice of these symbols. The Braille transcriber will therefore need to compile an appropriate list of Braille equivalents before the transcription of such a book is undertaken, and this list should be presented at the front of each volume in which the symbols occur. As a valuable aid to recognition by the Braille reader, each symbol in the list should be followed by its Braille dot numbers, enclosed in parentheses. The list should be prepared in consultation with the transcriber's supervisor or braille editor, since ease in reading is a most important factor in the choice of each Braille equivalent.

An example of such a list, which transcribers will find helpful as a model, is to be found in *Braille Textbook Formats and Techniques.*[24] In this list, the symbols each represent both the letter and the diacritic marking, and in use they are to be spaced in accordance with the print copy being transcribed. Reading is greatly facilitated if all words employing diacritics are written in contracted Braille.

Wherever possible, in systems where the letter and the diacritic marking are both included, the marking should precede the letter, even if it follows the letter in the print copy, or is written above or below it. The reading of braille is a strictly horizontal process, proceeding from left to right, and it therefore follows that reading is much easier if the reader is warned in advance of any diacritic or other modification, rather than finding it only after the letter to which it refers, or being obliged to search for it above or below the line of reading. It will be seen that this practice has been followed in the American example referred to above, except where the diacritic consists of letters joined together, in which case the print must be scrupulously followed. It is particularly important for accents or stress marks to precede the letter to which they refer, even when this is directly contrary to the practice of the print publisher.

Again for the sake of easy reading, diacritic stress marks should be substituted for capital letters, italics or other print methods of indicating stress.

Notes

1. N. I. Sundberg, 'UNESCO's Role in Promoting Educational, Scientific and Cultural Activities for the Blind in the Developing World', *Proceedings of the World Assembly of the World Council for the Welfare of the Blind (WCWB), São Paulo (Brazil), August 1974.*
2. P. Henri, 'General Summary of Work of the World Braille Council', *Proceedings of the World Assembly of the WCWB, Paris, August 1954,* p. 73.
3. Sir Clutha Mackenzie, 'Report of the Consultative Committee on Braille', *Proceedings of the World Assembly of the WCWB, New York, N.Y., August 1964,* p. 63.

4. P. Henri, 'Greater Uniformity in Braille Mathematics Symbols', *Proceedings of the World Assembly of the WCWB, Rome, July 1959.*

5. This was developed by Mr F. Rodrigo, Chairman, WCWB Subcommittee on Mathematics and Science, Organización Nacional de Ciegos, José Ortega y Gasset 18, Madrid 6 (Spain).

6. This was developed by Professor A. Nemeth, University of Detroit, 16240 Fairfield Avenue, Detroit, Mich. 48221 (United States).

7. Now Sri Lanka.

8. Mackenzie, op. cit., p. 62.

9. See, for example, Karl Britz, 'The German System of Contracted Braille : Some Critical Points of View', *AFB Research Bulletin,* No. 14, 1967.

10. See for example, V. Paske and J. Vinding, 'The "Perfect" Braille System', *AFB Research Bulletin,* No. 26, 1973, p. 135–8.

11. The rationale behind this project is described in : J. L. Douce and M. L. Tobin, 'Discussion Paper on the Desirability of a Joint Research Project on the Braille Code, Extending the Use of Braille, and the Improvement of Reading Skills', *Braille Automation Newsletter,* February 1976.

12. For example, G. F. Staack, *A Study of Braille Code Revisions* (M.S. Thesis, M.I.T.). (Abstract printed in *AFB Research Bulletin,* No. 2, 1962, p. 21–37).

13. C. J. Kederis, J. R. Siems and R. L. Haynes, 'A Frequency Count of the Symbology of English Braille Grade 2, American Usage', *International Journal for the Education of the Blind,* Vol. 15, December 1965, p. 38–46.

14. J. M. Gill and J. B. Humphreys, 'An Analysis of Braille Contractions', *Braille Research Newsletter,* No. 5, July 1977, p. 50–7.

15. J. M. Gill, *A Study of Braille Contractions,* p. 28-30. (Short paper distributed at the Workshop on Methods in Educational Research for the Blind, Uppsala (Sweden), September 1978.)

16. R. A. J. Gildea and M. Berkowitz, 'Computerized Braille', *Proceedings of a Workshop on Compliance of Computer Programs with English Braille, American Edition, New York City, 7-8 June 1976* (ACM and AFB 1977).

17. A. Nemeth, 'Evaluation of Staak's Recommended Revisions of the Braille Code', in Gildea and Berkowitz, op. cit., p. 56–7.

18. P. Duran, 'English Braille: Its Standardisation for Computers', Ibid., p. 113.

19. The following categorization is based on a personal communication, 29 November 1978, from F. Rodrigo, Chairman, WCWB Subcommittee on Mathematics and Science, Organización Nacional de Ciegos, José Ortega y Gasset 18, Madrid 6 (Spain).

20. Eric Blom (ed.), *Grove's Dictionary of Music and Musicians,* 5th ed., London, Macmillan. 10 vols.

21. World Council for the Welfare of the Blind (WCWB), *Revised International Manual of Braille Music Notation 1956. Part. 1: Western Music,* comp. by H.V. Spanner, Paris, 1956.

22. W. P. Merrick, W. Potthoff and D. Jones (comp.), *A Braille Notation of the International Phonetic Alphabet,* rev. ed., London, Royal National Institute for the Blind, 1948.

23. *A Code of Braille Textbook Formats and Techniques,* Louisville, Ky., American Printing House for the Blind, 1970.

24. *Braille Textbook Formats and Techniques,* p. 47, Louisville, Ky., American Printing House for the Blind, 1965.

Chapter 5

Reading, learning and teaching Braille

The nature of tactile reading

One commonly hears or reads about the superiority of vision over touch: that the eye is orders of magnitude more sensitive, greater in its capacity to deal with information, in its capacity to discriminate. Although these comparisons are not completely erroneous, the tactile sensory channel should not be regarded as so inferior.

Direct comparisons between visual and Braille reading show unambiguously that visual reading can take place at a significantly faster rate than Braille reading. Furthermore, the physical reading techniques are quite different. In visual reading, the eyes move in discrete 'jumps', fixating for short intervals in between. It is during these fixations that information is taken in from the printed page. In contrast, when the fingers are used for reading Braille, there should be a smooth, even movement of the finger(s) over the Braille characters in order that the sensory receptors in the fingertips can function efficiently.

Investigations of the visual and Braille reading process have produced two quite different models of the perceptual processes involved in these two types of reading. In visual reading, 'chunks' of text form the perceptual unit, i.e. the information taken in during a single 'eye-fixation'. Exactly how much text a 'perceptual chunk' corresponds to depends on a number of factors such as the complexity of the text and the skill of the reader. In Braille reading, it has been shown that the unit of perception is the character.[1] Thus, reading takes place by synthesizing the individual characters into meaningful wholes.

On a more theoretical level, however, there is some evidence to suggest that Braille reading does not exploit the tactile sensory channel optimally. For example, Kirman has argued that

there is considerable evidence that the maximum rate at which any sequence of familiar stimuli may be individually perceived in the correct order is in the range of about three to four per second. Such estimates have been obtained for visual stimuli ranging from non-linguistic stimuli to individual letters to whole phrases...., for non-linguistic as well as linguistic auditary stimuli… and for tactile stimuli… Assuming an average of five letters per English word, such an upper limit on the rate of perceptual processing would restrict the speed of any code which utilized the individual letter as the perceptual unit to below 36 to 48 words per minute. Uncontracted Braille, Moon type, Morse, the optophone, and letters visually presented one at a time are all within these predicted limits.

It is important to note that this limit of about three to four per second is not appreciably affected by the information content of the perceptual units… so that if words rather than letters could serve as perceptual units, reading rates could increase to between 180 to 240 words per minute. Obviously, if short phrases functioned as units, reading rates could go much higher, and current research indicates that in rapid reading, phrases do indeed function as perceptual units.[2]

This provides part of the rationale for having a contracted code system for Braille. However, there is an opposing influence restricting the extent of use of contractions, that is, increasing the amount of use made of contractions also increases the complexity of the code system. It has been argued that reading speed and efficiency are closely linked to the ability of the reader to use peripheral cues such as context, expectations and stored information during reading.[3] This cannot take place if the perception of the character system requires extended intellectual effort, as in the case with contracted Braille. Clearly the design of any contraction system must optimize between these two factors.

Given, however, the existence of an optimal code system, the perception of this system must allow the perceptual organization of relatively large perceptual units. Kolers has, however, pointed out that a possible reason for the difficulty with Braille is that 'the Braille system tries to map on a one-to-one basis for tactual reading the characteristics of print presented for visual reading.'[4] In other words, the characteristics of the print code have evolved to exploit the capacities of the visual system which, as described above, are quite different to the tactile system. In order to exploit the tactile system optimally, therefore, a form of stimulation specially designed for the way tactile information is perceived is required. Braille, no matter how it might be displayed, is never likely to fully exploit the perceptual capacity of the tactile sense. This is because the individual Braille characters making up a word are, configurationally, unrelated to one another and as a consequence no extended spatiotemporal pattern, essential for tactual 'chunking' of information into larger perceptual units, can emerge from their sequential presentation.[5]

From this theoretical viewpoint, the maximum reading speed even with optimally contracted Braille code would be somewhere below 180 words per minute. This assumes that reading proceeds by the sequential perception of each character in turn. Naturally it may be possible to exceed this maximum by guessing words before all the characters have been perceived.

At present Braille reading speeds are considered good if they approach 100 words per minute. Furthermore, many people fail to master Braille reading to a level which allows them to use it as a communication medium with any efficiency. There is, therefore, scope for investigating the learning and teaching of Braille on an applied level with the aim of allowing more people to gain access to, or make better use of, this medium.

Braille reading

Braille reading techniques

In order that tactile sensitivity of the fingers can be utilized to the full, their physical movement over the Braille characters should be smooth and even and the pressure on the dots light. Braille reading involves, therefore, developing skills of movement and co-ordination of the hands as well as discrimination and sensitivity of the tactile sense.

There have been a number of research studies on techniques of Braille reading[6] which, although not providing any absolutely clear evidence as to the best technique, have resulted in general agreement that 'the fastest readers are those who can sense Braille with either hand equally well and use both in partnership.'[7]

With regard to efficient hand use Caton et al. make the following recommendations based on research findings:

Lowenfeld & Abel[8] suggest placing the Braille book flat on a table or desk of comfortable height with the bottom edge of the book parallel to the reader's body and his two hands parallel to the surface of the book.

The fastest and best reading performance scores were achieved by students who read using the index fingers of both hands.[9] The most efficient way to find the next line while reading Braille is with the left hand while finishing the current line with the right.

Good readers read a considerable amount of material with the hands functioning independently, and the right hand covering approximately twice as much material alone as does the left hand alone. Apparently this independence does not develop naturally with reading experience, but must be taught.[10]

Studies have shown very good Braille readers tend to use constant low pressure while reading. More pressure is used when confronted with unfamiliar material.[11]

Despite the general agreement about the superiority of the techniques described above, studies show that their use is not as widespread as one might expect. Lorimer has summarized the conclusions from these studies as follows.

(a) Relatively few children are able to use both hands independently, but they are generally the best readers; (b) the majority depend largely or entirely on one hand for sensing braille characters, there being rather more dependence on the right hand than the left; (c) children who rely mainly on the left hand are rather more numerous among the poorer readers; (d) there appears to be no clear connection between hand preference in reading and handedness in other activities.[12]

This situation suggests that much greater emphasis should be placed on teaching and developing efficient hand techniques within any Braille teaching programme.

Perception of Braille

A good proportion of our knowledge about the processes involved in Braille reading originate from a series of studies carried out by Nolan and Kederis at the American

Printing House for the Blind. Their investigations consisted of nine experimental studies. These deal successively with the questions of the perceptual unit in word recognition, factors in the recognition of Braille characters, the process of word recognition and developmental factors in word recognition.

One of their main findings was 'that "whole-word" reading is not characteristic of the Braille readers studied and that the perceptual unit in word recognition is the Braille cell'.[13] Evidence for this comes from their specially constructed tachistacto-meter—a tactile analogue of the tachistoscope. They found that it took longer to recognize Braille words than the time calculated by adding up the recognition times of the individual characters. The opposite effect, i.e. word recognition times are less than the synthetic recognition times of the letters comprising that word, is found in visual tachistoscope experiments. This extra time in recognizing Braille words was believed to be spent 'integrating the information derived from the recognition of the individual characters'.[14]

The amount of time required to recognize a word seemed to be inversely related to the familiarity of the word, and to whether the word was contracted or uncontracted. These are not simple effects, however, as they are confounded by each other, and by other variables such as word length and the ability of the reader.

Factors influencing the recognition of Braille characters were extensively investigated. Two critical factors were isolated—number of dots in the Braille cell and their configuration. Although the precise way in which these interact has not really been sorted out, Nolan and Kederis give an interesting analysis of these two factors in terms of the types of recognition errors. The most frequent kind of error—missed dots—only occurred within 3-, 4-, and 5-dot characters. Furthermore, practically all the other error types occurred within the 3-dot characters. As it is only this group of 3-, 4-, and 5-dot characters which have what could be considered as shape, Nolan and Kederis argue that there is a probability relationship which leads the reader to have a greater expectancy that a character will have 3 dots. Their argument is worth reproducing here:

Specifically, to the 5-dot characters a dot cannot be added and the shape retained, and among the 4- and 3-dot characters the number of alternatives or chances of symbols being similar in shape is greater by a factor of three to one in the group of characters having fewer dots. For example, the 'q' character (⠟) which contains five dots, has within it a 'p' (⠏), a four dot character, and an 'm' (⠍) and 'f' (⠋) and a 'ff' (⠖), which are three dot characters. . . . Thus, if the reader is unsure of the Braille stimulus, he has a greater probability of being correct by naming one of these three-dot characters than a character of more dots.[15]

A further factor influencing the legibility of the Braille cell is the position of the dots within the cell. Their results indicated a tendency to favour the upper and left-hand portion of the Braille cell. They give a number of factors which might influence this, although they suggested the most important factor was likely to be the probability features of Braille. Kederis et al. found from a frequency count a bias towards the upper and left side dots as regards frequency of occurrence.[16]

The model of Braille reading that Nolan and Kederis put up is a 'sequential integrative' one, although they do point out that there are exceptions to this conclusion, for example, 'in many instances, words are correctly identified before all the characters are touched [and that] frequency of occurrence of various structural and grammatical elements of language, in all likelihood, also play a role in word recognition'.[17]

Several factors were isolated in these studies that effect the time required to recognize words. The general conclusion was that 'recognition times for Braille words become greater with decrease in familiarity, inclusion of contractions, increase in length, and shift in dot distributions from concentration in the upper parts of words'.[18] Usually the interaction of these variables augmented their effects, but again these were complex interactions yet to be fully sorted out—for example, the interaction between familiarity and orthography. In the case of familiar words, contractions aided recognition; however, the situation is reversed in the case of unfamiliar words.

The findings of Nolan and Kederis suggest a fundamentally different perceptual process for Braille reading to that found with visual reading. An important question is whether this is due simply to the physical characteristics of the finger and the type of stimulation Braille characters cause or whether the actual processing capacity of the tactile channel is the limiting factor.

There have been a number of studies relevant to this question. One carried out by Troxel compared visual and tactile reading in controlled modes of presentation.[19] In his first set of experiments, visual reading speeds were measured for two modes of presentation—letter by letter and word by word. In the word by word presentation, the display time was proportional to the number of letters in the word. The results show a 'reading' speed of 19.5 words per minute for the letter by letter presentation and 108.5 words per minute for the word by word presentation.

The tactile modes of presentation were far from ideal. For letter by letter presentation, solenoid-operated air valves were used to stimulate six positions on either one finger or one on each of six fingertips. For word-by-word presentation a stenotype machine was used in 'reverse'. That is words were fed into a stenotype machine such that the stenotype keys normally used to code the words fell away from the subject's fingers. The experimental subject was a stenotype student familiar with the stenotype code. The results obtained were an average letter-by-letter rate of 18 words per minute and a word-by-word rate of 44 words per minute.

Tactile reading rates of approximately 18 words per minute for letter by letter presentations compare favourably with the average rate of 19.5 words per minute obtained by visual letter by letter presentations. The average word at a time tactile rate of 44 words per minute was somewhat lower than the corresponding visual rate of 108.5 words per minute, but this is not surprising if we consider that random word lists were used for the tactile tests and ordinary English text was used for the visual tests. It is interesting to note also that, towards the end of the practice sessions with the tactile word by word presentations, the subject increased her speed markedly and it appeared that she began to respond to the *pattern*, rather than to the collection of individual characters.

Despite the several deficiencies of this experiment, the results do point towards the possibility that 'performance through the tactile and visual senses is comparable when the information presentation is restricted either to letter by letter or a word at a time. The principal limitation to information intake appears to be cognition and not the sensory channel that is employed'.[20]

A number of experiments have indicated that the regular grapheme-phoneme correspondences form the unit of perception for the visual reading process.[21] Pick et al. carried out a study to see if grapheme-phoneme correspondences are also utilized in a similar fashion by Braille readers.[22]

Legally blind Braille readers (aged 9–21) were used for the experiment. They were not, however, controlled for age of onset of blindness or years they had been reading Braille. Like the experiments using print, Pick, Thomas and Pick found that it took longer to spell out unpronounceable pseudo-words than it did pronounceable ones. They also found a consistent trend towards more errors in unpronounceable pseudo-words and that these errors were usually of a nature that made them more pronounceable. They concluded, therefore, the grapheme-phoneme correspondences functioned in Braille in the same way as they do in print.

Furthermore, studies carried out by Bliss et al.[23] and Foulke and Warm[24] on tactile information processing indicate that information is processed in essentially the same way independently of whether the incoming information is visual or tactile.

Although there are a number of shortcoming to the experiments described above, there does seem to be some evidence that it is not the tactile sensory channel itself which is the limiting factor for tactile information. This conclusion would lend support to the argument presented earlier that the limitations of Braille reading lie in the nature of the type of stimulation which Braille characters present to the fingers.

There have been, nonetheless, numerous attempts to increase Braille-reading rate and some very ambitious claims have been made. The next section will discuss some of the research which has been carried out.

Improving Braille-reading rate

There have been two distinct approaches reported in the literature regarding the increasing of Braille-reading rates. One involves the training and improvement of character recognition, the argument being if Braille involves the sequential integration of individual Braille characters, then, by increasing the speed of recognition of these characters, reading should proceed correspondingly faster. The other approach involves improving the way, and increasing the rate, of moving the fingers over the Braille page. The technique is based on rapid visual reading techniques, and assumes that a totally different tactual perceptual process can be learnt.

Before discussing these two approaches, it will be useful to look at what Braille-reading rates have actually been found to be. Table 1 summarizes Braille-reading rates reported in a number of research studies.

The most noticeable aspect about these reading speeds is their wide range. This is probably as much to do with the lack of any consistent method or test for the assessment of Braille-reading speed as it is with actual range of ability. Nevertheless, it seems that a reading speed of around 70 words per minute can be expected from an

Table 1. Braille-reading rates as reported in research

Study	Number and age group	Reading rate (wpm)	Remarks
Meyers et al. 1958	275 Grade 5–12	68	
	Grade 5–8	63	
	Grade 9–12	86	
	167 Adults	90	
Foulke et al. 1962	21 Grade 6–8	57	Science
	21 Grade 6–8	70	Literary
Nolan 1966	64 Grade 4–6	50	Science
	61 Grade 9–12	65	Science
	68 Grade 4–6	51	Social studies
	53 Grade 9–12	74	Social studies
Henderson 1967	12 Grade 3–6	73	Oral pre-treatment
	12 Grade 3–6	84	Oral post-treatment
Lowenfeld et al. 1969	50 Grade 4	84	Local school
	50 Grade 4	72	Residential school
	50 Grade 8	149	Local school
	50 Grade 8	116	Residential school
Gray and Todd 1968	277 Adults	81	Simple prose text
Williams 1971	488 11 years	78	195 (40%) excluded, as failed
	16 years	103	to attain a speed of 40 wpm.
Lorimer 1972	Total school population between 7 and 14 years		Standardization of Neale analysis of reading ability, Braille
	8 years	16	version.
	12 years	46	

Source: Research papers.[25]

average Braille reader. This speed probably represents a speed approximately one-third to one-half of that of print reading.

With regard to increasing reading rate through improving Braille character recognition, a number of studies have been carried out. Henderson investigated two groups of twelve subjects each, equated on sex, mean grade level, age, IQ and silent reading achievement.[26] The latter was assessed under motivated conditions (monetary reward) in order to obtain a pre-treatment score which represented maximum ability and to stabilize the motivation factor throughout the study.

The experimental group was given an eighteen-day programme, on an individual basis, which involved instruction to overcome errors in character identification plus practice to increase speed of recognition. The materials consisted of twenty different lists of Braille characters each containing a random order of the fifty-five single-cell Braille characters.

Results of the post-treatment tests, which involved measures of rate and accuracy of character recognition, oral reading, and rate and comprehension of silent reading, showed significant reductions in errors (83 per cent) and time (40 per cent) for character recognition. In oral reading, a 15 per cent increase in speed and a 28 per cent decrease of errors were shown and were also statistically significant. In silent reading, although the gains of the post-test were not statistically significant, they were in the direction of the experimental group. It was suggested that the results of the latter measure might have been adversely affected because of overstimulation due to the monetary awards.

A similar experiment has been carried out by Umsted.[27] He used thirty-six subjects in both experimental and control groups and all contractions of grade 2 Braille were presented.

He found statistically significant improvements in accuracy and speed. Further-more, silent reading speed was increased by twenty-nine words per minute (30 per cent) over the pre-test levels.

Similar results, although statistically non-significant, have also been obtained by Flanigan and Joslin,[28] and Nolan and Kederis.[29] These results give support to the model of Braille reading based on the character as the perceptual unit.

The other approach which has been taken to try to increase Braille reading rates has been to manipulate the 'rate of perception' of the Braille characters. One of the first reported findings of such 'display manipulation' was that of Grunwald, obtained while investigating the characteristics of a moving page display of Braille which he was developing.[30] This device allowed sheets of paper embossed with Braille characters to be moved at a known rate under the fingertips. Using three different types of text—random words, text from a high school biology test, and meaningless binary dot patterns (e.g., dot/dot; dot/blank, etc.), he determined the maximum speed at which the subjects were still able to pronounce the words, read the text, and perceive the presence or absence of the dot patterns respectively.

All these three measures gave the same number for the maximum sweep rate of the dots moving under the fingers for all subjects with reliable scores. This sweep rate was 13.8 cm per second, which is equivalent to 22 Braille characters per second, or (from statistical analysis of the texts used) 320 words per minute. From these findings Grunwald suggested that Braille could be perceived dynamically—the reader perceiving patterns in time, rhythms, rather than geometrical patterns in space.

Other studies specifically to investigate possibilities to increase reading rate through 'display manipulation' have been carried out by Flanigan and by Stockton.[31] Reading rate was paced through adjustment of the rate of presentation of Braille in the form of a continuous belt. Both reported significant increases in reading rates.

Kederis, Nolan and Morris, also using a variable speed continuous belt display, did not find any overall significant increase in reading rate for the children tested.[32] There was some evidence, however, that superior readers increased speeds when trained on such a display. As Nolan and Kederis point out, however, the 'most impressive finding was that through manipulation of motivational variables, reading speeds could be increased up to 100 per cent with no loss of comprehension. This finding casts doubt on the results of Flanigan and Stockton who left motivational variables uncon-trolled.'[33]

Foulke has also approached this question of increasing reading rate. In a preliminary investigation using a moving belt display he found that

comparison of the times needed for the identification of words with the sums of the times needed for the identification of the characters with which those words are composed indicated that, in many instances, whole words were identified in significantly less time than the sums of the identification times for the characters in those words. This result may be inconsistent with the result reported by Nolan & Kederis, although further experimentation and analysis will be required to clarify the issue. Our result was observed in the performance of the faster Braille readers in the experiment. It is reasonable to assume that faster Braille readers find reading a more rewarding experience and that they have, as a consequence, done a good deal more reading. Their greater background of experience in reading may have enabled them to predict some of the letters in words with greater success than the slow readers. To the extent that successfully predicted letters do not have to be identified, the words in which they occur may be identified more quickly. However, there is another possible explanation of our result. With experience, some Braille readers may learn a kind of perceptual 'chunking' that permits them, in many cases, to treat whole words as unitary patterns. This perceptual ability should significantly reduce the time needed for the identification of chunked words, with rapid Braille reading as a consequence.[34]

If the latter explanation is valid, then this, together with the claims made by Grunwald, argues against the research evidence presented by Kirman[35] who claims that the maximum rate of sequential perception of individual characters is about three to four per second. This is in contrast to twenty-two characters per second claimed by Grunwald. Clearly this disagreement of perceptual rates should be further investigated in an attempt to sort out exactly what the maximum rate of perception really is.

A somewhat different approach has attracted considerable attention during the past few years. This concentrates on the actual reading techniques used by the reader and perhaps as, if not more, important the motivation of the reader to read faster. The development of this method has been largely associated with McBride.[36]

This method of 'speed-reading' in Braille is directly analogous to 'speed-reading' in print. The training usually involves going through a structured training procedure which McBride has described as follows:

Step 1: Be enthusiastic and remain convinced that you *can* increase your reading rate . . .

Step 2: Secure a timing device . . .

Step 3: Have on hand several easy reading books . . .

Step 4: Have someone time you to see how fast you can encounter all of the words on one page. . . . Move your hands over the page in any manner you wish, i.e. across the page, straight down, straight up, spiraling, zig-zagging, etc. Try to use both hands and as many fingers as you can. . . .

Step 5: Now have your helper time you for 15 to 20 seconds as you move from page to page rapidly, again with no comprehension and attempting to not say the words in your mind. . . .

Step 6: Continue this process for two days, experimenting often with new hand . . . movements. . . . Try to go faster each time, again without saying the words in your mind.

Step 7: Go over the same pages again and again. On the third day of practice, begin to try to understand some of the words. . . . Do not try to understand more than two or three words on a page.

Step 8: Remember, you are going over the same material again and again. . . . Continue this until you begin to get a little sense out of the story. . . . In this process (after about two hours of 'bits and pieces' (see Step 7)) you might feel that you need to slow down a little to understand better.

Step 9: Begin each practice session with 'warm up' exercises, i.e. two or three runs of 20–60 seconds for 'speed only' with no comprehension. Then move into comprehension, trying for more comprehension each day. Move into more difficult books now, books which have more words per page. . . . do not chose the most difficult yet. Increase the level of difficulty only as you feel you should. . . . Flexibility becomes important now. Adjust your rate to suit your needs. . . .

Step 10: You may wish to change the position of your reading materials to accommodate your particular way of reading. . . .

Step 11: Begin now to think in terms of 'main ideas', 'sequence of ideas', 'main characters', and the relationship of the main characters to the story. . . . Work for 'book report' comprehension.[37]

As a result of following these procedure, McBride has claimed that the average Braille reading speed of the members of one of his workshops increased from 138 words per minute to 710 words per minute. These rates were determined using informal tests of reading performance.

An examination of McBride's procedures has been carried out by Olson et al.[38] by examining the data from three workshops for speed reading; one taught by McBride and the other two, one of which was for large print readers, by one of his researchers. In the Braille groups, informal post-tests showed a reading rate of 275 words per minute (an increase of 177 words per minute over the pre-test scores) and 203 words per minute (an increase of 126 words per minute over the pre-test scores). Variations within each group were, however, extremely large—pre-test rates ranging from 24 to 163 words per minute and 20 to 250 words per minute in the two Braille groups, and post-tests rates ranging from 100 to 855 words per minute and 30 to 477 words per minute. Formal testing, using Diagnostic Reading Scales, also showed a significant increase in rate, although rather less spectacular.[39] For one of the Braille groups, average reading rate increased from 79 to 120 words per minute and for the other from 93 to 121 words per minute. Variations were also large in the formal testing results. With regard to comprehension, no significant change took place when measured formally.

One interesting finding was that, although there was no difference between informal and formal pre-test measures, a difference was found between the post-test measures. As Olson et al. point out 'it is possible that the substantially greater rates on the informal post-test were achieved because of lower comprehension levels. In an attempt to read faster, readers may not have been truly reaching the estimated 'book report' level of 80 per cent comprehension. Another explanation for the discrepancy between post-test measures of rate might be that each test evoked a different kind of reading. The rapid reading training may have, in fact, taught individuals to suppress the unimportant words on a page as their ... fingers passed over them. While the informal testing may have enhanced this kind of reading, it is logical to assume that the formal test situation might diminish this ability by causing readers to "search" for possible test items.'[40]

This illustrates a critical aspect of 'speed reading' studies—how is reading performance evaluated? It would appear from the above that the claims for very high speeds are based on only informal assessment of reading, with no real check on comprehension. Furthermore, comprehension measurement, tested formally, might be based on significantly lower reading speeds.

With regard to increasing Braille reading rates, it seems that improvements can be made by code recognition training and by learning new techniques of hand movement and of 'reading' itself.

The concept of reading in fact seems quite a central issue in discussions of speed reading. McBride claims that 'I do not believe that we teach real reading in school. I believe, rather, that we teach *slow* reading in school. Real reading is *faster* reading....'[41] It would be easy, however, to claim the opposite—that 'real' reading is thorough reading and understanding of a text which, in print as well as in Braille, usually occurs at a slower rate, and certainly well within a person's capacity. Speed reading, one might claim, only encourages a superficial comprehension of the text and does not allow the reader to reflect on the author's ideas.

The point here is not to suggest that a certain type of reading should be practised *instead* of another. Rather the particular advantages of one approach over another for particular types of material in particular situations should be made clear. Furthermore, with respect to speed reading the critical importance of motivation, personality and general approach to unconventional ways of doing things should be emphasized.

Learning to read Braille

Factors involved in the learning-to-read situation are numerous and are particularly so if the medium being learnt is Braille. These factors will be discussed in two groups, those dependent on the reader, and those dependent on the medium, i.e. the Braille system itself.

Learning factors relating to the reader

Age/age of onset of handicap

Lorimer has found from standardizing the Neale Test of Reading Ability that of 'children able to learn Braille, the more able will probably be able to begin a little before the age of 7 while the less able are unlikely to make headway in reading before they are 8 years old. The progress of even better readers is somewhat slow until just after the age of 9, and it is only at about the age of 11 that they appear to have mastered the mechanics of reading and are able to use Braille as a medium for learning. The poorer readers, on the other hand, are constantly lagging far behind and are far from competent even at the age of 12.'[42]

The reasons for this falling behind, Lorimer suggests, are partly to do with the complexities of the Braille code but 'probably even more to the fact that blind children generally are slower than sighted children in developing skills basic to reading readiness [and] it may be ... that the perceptual difficulty so noticeable in the early stages of learning to read arises from the fact that maturation of tactual and motor skills is still under way and is insufficient for making the fine touch perceptions and hand and finger movements needed for reading Braille.'[43]

With regard to learning Braille when older, there appears to be some conflicting evidence. From the survey by Gray and Todd a strong relationship was shown between age of onset of visual handicap and learning Braille. A marked decrease in the numbers learning Braille and becoming good enough to read occurred after the age of 29. The older groups, comment Gray and Tood, are 'by reason of age, probably less adept, physically and mentally, at learning a completely new method of reading by touch.'[44]

This is in contrast to a finding of Tobin's from an investigation of factors underlying the ability to learn Braille in former readers of inkprint.[45] His subjects (thirty-one men, thirteen women) were drawn from a rehabilitation centre for the blind and persons resident in their own houses. Their ages ranged from 20 to 80 years with an average of 49 years. The object of the investigation was to study some different variables in the design of a self-instructional programme for Braille reading. One of his findings was that there was no significant correlation between age and reading performance at the end of the instructional programme. It should be emphasized, however, that all subjects were well past adolescence.

The explanation of this difference may partly lie however, in motivational factors and implies that newly blinded adults should not be denied Braille reading instruction by reason of age alone. Support for this conclusion can be found in recent increases in Braille readership in Sweden which have been partly the result of a greater concentration on Braille instruction in rehabilitation centres for newly blind adults.

Intelligence

It is generally agreed that intelligence is an even more important factor influencing Braille reading performance than it is for print reading. For example, Mommers has found that 'poor Braille readers, relatively speaking, lie further behind the poor sighted readers than the good Braille readers lie behind the good sighted readers';[46] a finding reinforcing that of Nolan and Kederis[47] that the base level of intelligence required for Braille reading may be much higher than that for inkprint reading.

Lorimer has also found that a consistent difference of about 20 IQ points separated children at all age levels between 8 and 12 in the upper and lower thirds of reading accuracy and rate as measured by the Neale test.[48] All but two of the children, furthermore, at the age of 8 had IQs of 100 or more.

Tactual perception

With regard to tactual and kinesthetic abilities, a number of studies have been carried out, mainly with the aim of investigating their predictive ability for Braille reading performance. Nolan and Morris found significant correlations between the ability to discriminate different degrees of roughness and reading speeds and errors in young blind children.[49] Tobin developed a 'touch test' using a simple punctiform (non-Braille) stimulus which must be matched against five similar figures, only one of which being exactly similar.[50] Although the test proved to be statistically significant with regard to validity coefficient (similar to that obtained by Nolan and Morris for their Roughness Discrimination Test), Tobin doubted the usefulness of such a test alone in predicting Braille reading ability.

In a correlational analysis of intelligence, haptic or tactile perception and Braille reading, Mommers found that haptic form discrimination and haptic figure orientation are more closely related to reading than haptic size and roughness discrimination.[51]

Language ability

As one would intuitively expect, there is a significant relationship between language (as measured by verbal intelligence) and reading achievement. More directly, a number of studies have shown that contextual cues in texts, for example, grammatical structures, certain word endings, familiar letter sequences, etc., aid the reading process considerably.[52] Ability to utilize these linguistic cues clearly depends on the reader's level of language development.

In the case of the visually handicapped, some writers have suggested that lack of vision will have a significant influence on their language development and use. Exactly what kind of influence, however, does not seem to be agreed upon. Tobin argues that 'on the one hand, visual handicap is seen as in some way retarding the full elaboration of language . . . on the other hand, as serving as an important eagerly used tool for defining the child and his world.'[53] He tentatively concludes that with regard to language development, parity with the sighted is eventually reached but the process is on the whole slower, although the best of the blind will at all ages compare favourably with the best of the sighted.

This implies that at a given age there is likely to be greater variations in the language ability of visually handicapped children than among their sighted peers. This is an aspect which has considerable implications for the teaching of Braille reading and especially for the development of beginners' reading materials. These will be discussed in the section dealing with the teaching of Braille.

Learning factors relating to the medium

Discrimination of Braille characters

A child born blind is, or at least should be, taught to use his tactual sense for fine discrimination from a very young age. Thus, for an otherwise normal child, the actual discrimination of Braille characters does not usually present a large problem. For people losing their sight later in life, however, the perceptual factor grows more and more difficult with age. For this reason, use of an 'expanded' Braille cell has been advocated by some teachers.

From Tobin's investigation of Braille reading in former readers of inkprint,[54] a division of opinion was revealed between reading teachers on this question of use of an expanded Braille cell. In a subsequent investigation of this question, he found that a teaching programme using an expanded cell (together with using contracted Braille from the beginning; another point of division between teachers) resulted in the best results in the initial stages of learning. The influence of cell size is, however, relatively small compared to individual differences between learners.

Code system

In Braille systems which use a complex rule system governing the use of Braille contractions (e.g. English, German, etc.), the extra complexities of the contraction system could retard reading development and cause a higher failure rate among learners.

One of the main difficulties arising out of a contracted code system is the reduction of the 'redundancy' in the text. Briefly, redundancy is a measure of the 'surplus information' present in the text over and above that which is strictly necessary. For example, few English-speaking people will have trouble in guessing the following words: TEA__ER, INDU__RY, FA__ORY. This shows that words usually contain more letters (i.e., 'information') than they strictly need for identification. In fact, it can be shown that English is 66 per cent redundant, i.e. it should be possible to transmit the same amount of information using the same alphabet, but with 66 per cent fewer letters.

When print is transcribed into grade 2 Braille, however, a great deal of this redundancy is lost. For example, the English words 'letter' and 'little' are spelt 'lr' and 'll' in grade 2 Braille. Thus, these words which differ by three letters in print only differ by one letter in Braille. Furthermore, the Braille character for 'r' (⠗) and 'l' (⠇) differ by only one dot. Thus, these two words in Braille are much more likely to be confused than they are in print. This situation increases the burden on the learner, particularly in the initial stages when perceptual factors are very great.

Teaching Braille reading

Up until the present time, the teaching of Braille has borrowed the conventional techniques and materials used for the teaching of print reading. During the 1970s, however, there was an increasing awareness that teaching Braille, and especially where a contracted Braille system exists, requires material specially developed so as to take account of the complexities and difficulties imposed by the Braille system.

Before considering these aspects specific to Braille, a brief overview of approaches to the teaching of print reading will be given as these still form the basis for teaching Braille.

Teaching the sighted to read: some relevant aspects

Until fairly recently, the teaching of reading in ordinary schools took one of two emphases. Either a 'whole-word' or a 'meaning' approach was pursued, or alternatively, a 'phonic' approach.

At the beginning of Chall's examination of the methods and research in teaching the reading of print, she gave eight principles which briefly outline the point of view of the 'meaning' or 'whole-word' approach to teaching reading. They are as follows:

1. The process of reading should be defined broadly to include as major goals, *right from the start*, not only word recognition, but also comprehension and interpretation, appreciation and application of what is read, to the study of personal and social problems.
2. The child should start with 'meaningful reading' of whole words, sentences, and stories as closely geared to his own experiences and interests as possible. Silent reading should be stressed from the beginning.
3. After the child recognises 'at sight' about fifty words ... he should then begin to study, through analysing words 'learned as wholes' the relationship between the sounds in spoken words (phonemes) and the letters representing them (graphemes), i.e. phonics. However, *even before* instruction in phonics is begun, *and after*, the child should be encouraged to identify new words by picture and meaning clues. Structural analysis should begin about the same time as phonics and should be continued longer.
4. Instruction in phonics and other means of identifying words should be spread over the six years of elementary school. Usually, instruction in phonics is started slowly in grade 1, gathering momentum in grades 2 and 3.
5. Drill or practice in phonics 'in isolation' should be avoided; instead, phonics should be integrated with the meaningful connected reading. In addition, the child should not isolate sounds and blend them to form words. Instead, he should identify unknown words through a process of visual analysis and substitution.
6. The words in the pupil's readers for grades 1, 2 and 3 should be repeated often. They should be carefully controlled on a meaning-frequency principle, i.e. they should be the words that appear most frequently in general reading matter and that are within the child's listening and speaking vocabulary.
7. The child should have a slow and easy start in the first grade. All the children should go through a readiness or preparatory period, and those not judged ready for formal reading instruction should have a longer one.
8. Children should be instructed in small groups ... selected on the basis of their achievement in reading.

Chall goes on to say that all these principles have been challenged by advocates of the phonics approach; this alternative will now be discussed.

A 'phonics' approach, in fact, covers a multitude of differing methods. The most important thing that they have in common is that they emphasize the fact that language is a code, with rules, and a knowledge of these rules must precede being able to read.

The phonic approach originated in the learning of the alphabet. Syllables were learned by spelling out the letters, then words were learned, again by spelling them out. The underlying assumption of this approach was that the difficulty of learning the pronunciation of letter combinations is directly related to the number of letters combined. This organization of letters, syllables and words later became constructed around their sounds rather than just number of units.

There are two different approaches within the general framework of a phonics approach. One, the *synthetic,* is the more traditional conception of a phonics approach. It involves learning the sounds of the letters, and then synthesizing these sounds to build up word sounds. A more modern phonic approach is one that involves a more *analytic* approach. As such, it involves the analysis of words, introduced according to a preconceived order so as to emphasize the regularity of certain language patterns. The rationale is that the child can then apply his knowledge of those language patterns to identify new words.

Chall showed that research from 1912 to 1965 indicates that 'the code emphasis method produces better results'.[55] However, she also emphasizes strongly that 'the evidence does not endorse any one code-emphasis method over another [and] I recommend a code-emphasis method only as a beginning reading method—a method to start the child on—and that I do *not* recommend ignoring reading for meaning practice.' Also clear from her recommendations is that a good teacher is as essential as a good method, and that where a teacher has success with a particular method, that method is good in the situation no matter what the results of reading research might suggest.

Current methods for teaching Braille reading

Lowenfeld, Abel and Hatlen conducted a survey of Braille reading instruction in the United States during 1965.[56] This survey was based on teachers of blind children in residential and non-residential schools. A considerable consensus of opinion was found regarding methods of teaching Braille reading. 'The replies showed, with striking similarity, that in local schools as well as in residential schools 64% begin with whole words and/or meaningful sentences, and only 36% begin by using the Braille alphabet . . ., 96% of the residential schools and 94% of the local schools answered that they are using Braille grade II'. Many of the teachers indicated that they shift to the word method as soon as the children have learned sufficient letters to permit this.

This emphasis on the whole-word approach would seem to indicate a direct transference of methods used for teaching print reading to teaching Braille reading. The findings of Nolan and Kederis that Braille is read sequentially, unlike print, suggest that a better approach might be to concentrate on Braille character recognition.[57]

With regard to finger use, the survey by Lowenfeld et al. showed that two-thirds of residential school teachers and about one-third of local school teachers encouraged the use of the index fingers of both hands.[58] The remaining teachers encouraged the use of various other finger combinations or left it to the children to use the fingers they prefer.

The studies by Tobin and Norris provide a fairly clear picture of teaching Braille reading in the United Kingdom. There, teachers tend, by and large, to evolve their own individual methods of teaching Braille reading, and, as a consequence, a few schools have their own reading scheme.

Norris's survey showed that three out of seven schools taught grade II from the beginning, one school began with grade I progressing to grade II when children became familar with the letters, one school taught a selective grade II, and two schools had no policy as regards grade of Braille taught first. Norris points out, however, that 'not all teachers understand the same thing by the term "grade II Braille". . . . Very few teachers follow what might be termed a complete grade II system, where the child learns to read only whole words in their contracted forms from the very beginning'.[59]

Tobin's study was to devise a 'self-instructional programme . . . to enable newly blinded adolescent and adult persons to learn Braille in the absence of a regular teacher [and also] it was hoped that through the use of survey, correlational, and experimental methods, some light might be thrown on the relative value of differing teaching approaches and on the importance of various "organismic" variables...'.[60] This study, or rather series of studies, differs from most of the previous work done in this area as it concerns newly-blinded who have already learnt print before the onset of blindness.

The investigation consists of a number of studies including a survey of the current teaching methods used by both teachers in schools and the home teachers (who have since ceased to exist), some pilot studies to obtain information about the feasibility of a tactual discrimination test to obtain data on pre-Braille touch skills, and studies on the organismic variables in the learning of Braille.

The two main differences in teaching practices revealed by the survey were (a) starting with grade I or with grade I plus simple word signs, and (b) the use of expanded Braille cells to start with, i.e. using Braille cells with the interdot spacing larger than the conventional 0.09 inches. The studies conducted to evaluate these differences showed that 'the combination of a contracted form of Braille and large cell configuration leads to higher levels of performance in the initial stages of learning'.

However, as Tobin points out in his discussion, 'individual differences among learners are such that the methods used by their teachers are unlikely to account for more than a relatively small proportion of the observed variability . . . a teacher strongly committed to a particular approach is likely to make it work, even if there is an alternative that is somewhat better'.[61] This is not to suggest that all research on the teaching of reading is worthless. What it does is to emphasize the importance of eliciting the variables in the teaching situation and evaluating their effectiveness.

Development of beginning reading materials

Rex carried out a study on four basal reading series used for the teaching of Braille reading.[62] These were standard books and so had been written without consideration of the use of the Braille code.

Her results indicated that: 165 contractions of the 189 in the (American) literary code were used, 131 of which were used by all four (60 per cent of the total contractions used were introduced in the four series by the end of the first grade); and the average new contractions per word rate ranged from one every two words, at pre-primer level, to one every fifty at grade 3 level. This is the obvious consequence of introducing most of the contractions early on. The cumulative frequency of appearance of all the contractions was between one for every 1.6 words to one for every 2.1 words. The four reading series showed great consistency for these measures.

Rex points out some dangers of using such reading series. For example, the confusability of certain Braille characters are not controlled for. The sequential pattern of some word recognition skills, such as the phonemic elements of words, is distorted when words are contracted, and the basal reader does not provide adequate instructional material to deal with the special aspects of the Braille code. This study clearly points out the need for teachers to examine critically standard reading series, and the data from her analyses does provide some guidelines for the design of new material.

Considerable effort was made during the 1970s to develop beginning reading material for Braille. A second stage of Rex's study described above was to develop experimental supplementary instructional material from her data.

Rex defined the special problems of the Braille code which would benefit from such supplementary material as being:

Dual spelling of words such as IN, WAS, TO which appear in both contracted and uncontracted form.

Multiple use of symbols, such as the use of the same symbol for punctuation marks and lower-cell contractions.

Similar configuration which occurs when lower-cell forms are used, and when the same symbols are used in both one-cell and two-cell contractions or similar two-cell contractions.

Rules of the code which are related to the above but are even more comprehensive when consideration must be given to such aspects as position of letters within a word or words within a sentence, syllabication, compostion signs, and various other features.

Non-phonetic aspects of the code which the use of contractions frequently imposes and which become even greater problems with the increasing use of phonics as an approach in reading instruction.

The material which Rex developed was a series of forty lessons, each consisting of about four Braille pages. Each lesson was designed to emphasize a particular concept within the Braille code and introduce a particular group of contractions, short form words, etc. Each lesson was designed along the lines of programmed instruction.

From a small pilot study conducted to evaluate this material, Rex found gains in the experimental group in the direction of improvement, but these were not statistically significant, although, as Rex points out, this was probably due to the fact that the experimental period was only eight weeks. Both Rex and the teachers involved in the study agreed that 'the presentation of concepts should extend over a longer period of time than eight weeks'. Some of the problems incurred in the development of such materials were selecting vocabulary, and defining and making clear the directions of use of the material to both teacher and child.

In the United Kingdom, a sub-committee of the College of Teachers of the Blind has produced a scheme for a beginning reading series called 'The Family Books'.[63] The words used in these books are selected from the Tobin vocabulary study [64] and the sub-committee decided upon the order of introduction of Braille signs. The actual stories, however, were written by the teachers themselves. The scheme is currently in use in several schools and has also been bought for children who are integrated into the normal school system. There has been no feedback however, as to how well the scheme stands up in unspecialized hands.[65]

At the American Printing House for the Blind, a major programme has been carried out '... to develop a set of beginning reading materials, specifically designed to minimize problems encountered by the beginning reader of Braille. The subordinate objectives of this programme were stated as follows:

To write detailed coordinated specifications for Braille readers, Braille workbook materials, and teacher's manuals using all relevant information from research on Braille reading and print reading.

To analyze common word lists to identify words to be used as vocabulary in specially designed Braille readers.

To write special Braille readers based on these specifications and vocabulary lists.

To write teachers' manuals meeting these specifications.

To submit all materials as developed to review by an expert committee and revise as required.[66]

This programme was carried out over three years and was completed in August 1978. The set of specifications used in order to develop the materials was based on a review of research in the areas of Braille reading, general tactile perception, development of concepts by blind children, and general practices in teaching reading. Vocabulary selection was based on standardized word lists (Dale 769 Easy Words and the Dolch Basic Sight Words).

The introduction of vocabulary was based on four factors. First, *categories of Braille code*—these categories are based on the difficulties children learning to read Braille have in the discrimination of words, characters or signs. In order of increasing difficulty these are: alphabet abbreviations; full spelling, upper-cell words and contractions; lower-cell words and contractions; combinations of orthography; and short-form words. Second, *individual characters of the Braille code*—these categories are based on the difficulties visually handicapped children have in the recognition of individual characters. These were used in conjunction with the categories presented above. These are, in order of difficulty, as follows: missed dot errors, ending problems, reversals, added dots, association errors, gross substitutions, vertical alignments and horizontal alignment. In addition the following factors should be considered: both order and magnitude of errors changed with grade level; reversals and substitutions decreased with grade; ending problems and association errors increased with age; and missed dots, added dots, vertical alignment and horizontal alignment remained fairly constant in rank.

Third, *frequency of errors*—these specifications contain information regarding Braille characters, words and clusters of characters which frequently present difficulties to students who read Braille. They are sub-divided into frequently confused characters and frequency of errors for clusters of characters. Fourth, *orders of difficulty*—this refers to orders of difficulty for the fifty-five one-cell characters of grade 2 Braille and for the contracted and uncontracted words in the Dale/Dolch Vocabulary List. These are categorized as follows: the fifty-five one-cell characters in order of difficulty based on number of errors; the fifty-five one-cell characters in order of difficulty based on recognition times; the fifty-five one-cell characters in order of number of dots; uncontracted words in order of number of dots per word (316 words from the Dale/Dolch list); and contracted words in order of number of dots per word (446 words from the Dale/Dolch list).

No specific teaching approach was identified as being the most acceptable for teaching Braille reading. Two approaches, which have been used with visually handicapped students are, however, described. These include two 'linguistic' approaches—the Progressive Part Braille Programme for Teaching Educationally Handicapped Blind Students and the Design for Introducing Reading in Braille to Multi-Impaired Visually Handicapped Children. A general description is given of the 'experience' approach; no specific programme is mentioned as none have been developed for visually handicapped children using this approach.

Finally, other topics relevant to teaching methodology are discussed, including concept development, reading instruction (implications for reading readiness and recommendations regarding teaching methods), hand use, reading rates, writing and formats for tactile materials.

A study recently reported investigated the extent to which a developmental programme of tactile perception and Braille letter recognition would effect errors in tactile perception, Braille letter recognition and undesirable scrubbing and backtracking behaviours of Braille users, as well as decrease the frequency of errors in Braille letter recognition.

1. Remedial Braille users who complete the developmental program will demonstrate significantly fewer undesirable scrubbing behaviors than will those not completing the program (controls).
2. Remedial Braille users who complete the developmental program will demonstrate significantly fewer undesirable backtracking behaviors than will those not completing the program.
3. Remedial Braille users who complete the developmental program will demonstrate significantly fewer undesirable errors in Braille recognition than will those not completing the program.
4. Subjects who are *introduced* to Braille via the developmental program will demonstrate significantly fewer undesirable scrubbing behaviors than will those not using the program (control).
5. Subjects who are *introduced* to Braille via the developmental program will demonstrate significantly fewer undesirable backtracking behaviors than will those not using the program.
6. Subjects who are *introduced* to Braille via the developmental program will demonstrate significantly fewer undesirable errors in Braille letter recognition than will those not using the program.[67]

Sixty-four students were tested. Fifteen matched pairs were selected using five criteria—date of birth, visual acuity, beginning or remedial Braille users, residential or state school placement, and pre-test scores. The subjects ranged in age from five to fifteen and included beginning Braille readers as well as pupils receiving extra Braille reading tuition. Students from seventeen state schools and residential schools were selected. Half of the sample was assigned at random to the experimental group and half to the control group and a pre-test, treatment, post-test design set. The experimental treatment consisted of tactile perception and Braille letter recognition, based on a model of precision teaching. The model used was an integral part of the Mangold Developmental Programme of Tactile Perception and Braille Letter Recognition.[68]

Ample time was provided so that each student could complete the entire programme; the time required for this ranged between six and sixteen weeks, with a median of thirteen weeks.

The results showed that those in the experimental group demonstrated significantly fewer errors in tactile perception and Braille letter recognition, and fewer undesirable backtracking and scrubbing behaviours.

In the discussion of her results, Mangold states:

The unique aspects of the program lie in the manner of adaptation into Braille, identification of a hierarchy of tactile perception, and the establishment of minimal performance goals for the 29 skills being taught. In addition, the precision teaching procedures allow for on-going student assessment which helps the teacher determine the appropriateness of her instruction.

Two points of interest revealed by the study were:

1. The developmental program was successfully used with 90 per cent of the remedial readers, who have had a history of reading difficulties. The program was equally successful with students across a wide age span of from 5 to 15 years.
2. The print teacher's manual includes an inkprint duplication of every Braille student worksheet.

This format was a major benefit of the developmental programme since it was found to be easily used by teachers and aides who had no formal instruction in Braille, as well as by teachers and aides who were familiar with the Braille system. This is a particularly important aspect of the programme since many visually impaired children are mainstreamed in state school programmes where they receive only periodic assistance from special teachers who know Braille.[64]

Notes

1. C. Y. Nolan and C. J. Kederis, *Perceptual Factors in Braille Word Recognition*, New York, N.Y., American Foundation for the Blind, 1969 (AFB Research Series, No. 20).
2. J. H. Kirman, 'Tactile Communication of Speech: A Review and an Analysis', *Psychological Bulletin*, Vol. 80, 1973, p. 54–74.
3. T. Mackworth, 'Some Models of the Reading Process in Learner or Skilled Readers', *Reading Research Quarterly*, Vol. 7, 1972, p. 701–33.
4. P. A. Kolers, 'Sensory Supplementation: Reading', in M. Graham (ed.), *Science and Blindness: Retrospective and Prospective*, New York, N.Y., American Foundation for the Blind, 1972.

5. Kirman, op. cit.

6. B. F. Holland, 'Speed and Pressure Factors in Braille Reading', *Teachers Forum,* Vol. 7, September 1934, p. 13–17; P. Fertsch, 'An Analysis of Braille Reading', *Outlook for the Blind and Teachers Forum,* Vol. 40, May 1946, p. 128–131; T. Kusajima, *Visual Reading and Braille Reading; AFB State of the Art Report,* New York, N.Y., American Foundation for the Blind, 1974.

7. J. Lorimer, *Outlines of a Short Course to Improve the Braille Reading Efficiency of Children in Lower Senior Classes.* Birmingham, Research Centre for the Education of the Visually Handicapped, 1977.

8. B. Lowenfield and G. L. Abel, *Methods of Teaching Braille Reading; Final Report,* San Francisco State College, February 1967. (Contract No. OE-5-10-009, Office of Education, US Department of Health, Education and Welfare.)

9. J. S. Lappin and E. Foulke, 'Expanding the Tactual Field of View', *Perception and Psychophysics,* Vol. 14, No. 2, 1973, p. 213–41.

10. Fertsch, op. cit.

11. Kusajima, op. cit.; H. Caton, E. Pester and S. Goldblatt, *Specifications for the Beginning Braille Reading Series,* Louisville, Ky., American Printing House for the Blind, 1978.

12. J. Lorimer, 'A Summary of Research in Braille Reading', *The Teaching of the Blind,* Vol. LX, No. 3, April 1972.

13. Holland, op. cit., p. 36.

14. Ibid, p. 84.

15. Ibid, p. 68.

16. C. J. Kederis, J. R. Siems and R. L. Haynes, 'A Frequency Count of the Symbology of English Braille Grade 2, American Usage', *International Journal for the Education of the Blind,* Vol. 15, December 1965, p. 38–46.

17. Nolan and Kederis, op. cit., p. 39.

18. Ibid, p. 41.

19. D. E. Troxel, 'Experiments on Tactile and Visual Reading', *IEEE Transactions on Human Factors in Electronics,* Vol. HFE-8, No. 4, December 1967.

20. Ibid.

21. E. J. Gibson, A. D. Pick, H. Osser and M. Hammond, 'The Role of Grapheme-Phoneme Correspondence in the Perception of Words', *American Journal of Psychology,* Vol. 75, 1962, p. 554–70; E. J. Gibson, H. Osser and A. D. Pick, 'A Study of the Development of Grapheme-Phoneme Correspondence', *Journal of Verbal Learning and Verbal Behavior,* Vol. 2, 1963, p. 142–6.

22. A. D. Pick, M. L. Thomas and H. L. Pick, 'The Role of Grapheme-Phoneme Correspondences in the Perception of Braille', *Journal of Verbal Learning and Verbal Behavior,* Vol. 5, 1966, p. 298–300.

23. J. Bliss, H. D. Crane, S. W. Link and J. T. Townsend, 'Tactile Perception of Sequentially Presenting Spatial Patterns', *Perception and Psychophysics,* Vol. 1, 1966, p. 125–36; J. Bliss, H. D. Crane and S. W. Link, 'Effect of Display Movement on Tactile Pattern Perception', *Perception and Psychophysics,* Vol. 1, 1966, p. 195–202; J. Bliss, H. D. Crane, P. K. Mansfield and J. T. Townsend, 'Information Available in Brief Tactile Presentation', *Perception and Psychophysics,* Vol. 1, 1966, p. 273–83.

24. E. Foulke and J. Warm, *The Development of an Expanded Reading Code for the Blind; Final Report to US Department of Health, Education and Welfare,* University of Louisville, 1968.

25. E. Meyers, D. Ethington and S. C. Ashcroft, 'Readability of Braille as a Function of Three Spacing Variables', *Journal of Applied Psychology,* Vol. 42, 1958, p. 163–5; E. Foulke, C. Amster, C. Y. Nolan and R. H. Bixler, 'The Comprehension of Rapid Speech by the Blind', *Exceptional Children,* Vol. 29, 1962, p. 131-41; C. Y. Nolan, 'Reading and Listening in Learning by the Blind', unpublished report, American Printing House for the Blind, 1966 (Progress Report, PHS Grant No. NB-04870-04); F. Henderson, 'The Effect of Character Recognition Training on Braille Reading', unpublished specialist in education thesis, George Peabody College for Teachers, 1967; B. Lowenfeld, G. Abel and P. Hatlen, *Blind Children Learn to Read,* Springfield, Ill., Charles C. Thomas, 1969; P. G. Gray and J. E. Todd, *Mobility and Reading Habits of the Blind; Government Social Survey (SS386),* London, HMSO; M. Williams, 'Braille Reading', *Teacher of the Blind,* Vol. LIX, No. 3, 1971, p. 103–16; J. Lorimer, 'A Summary of Research in Braille Reading', *The Teaching of the Blind,* Vol. LXI, No. 1, October 1972.

26. F. Henderson, 'The Rate of Braille Character Recognition as a Function of the Reading Process', *48th Proceedings of AAIB,* p. 7–10, 1966.

27. R. G. Umsted, 'Improving Braille Reading', *New Outlook for the Blind,* Vol. 66, No. 6, June 1972, p. 169–77.

28. P. Flanigan, E. Joslin, 'Patterns of Response in the Perception of Braille Configurations', *New Outlook for the Blind,* Vol. 63, 1969, p. 232–44.

29. Nolan and Kederis, op. cit.

30. A. P. Grunwald, 'On Reading and Reading Braille', *Proceedings of the Braille Research Development Conference, Cambridge, Mass., Sensory Aids Evaluation and Development Center, 1966.*

31. P. Flanigan, 'Automated Training and Braille Reading', *New Outlook for the Blind,* Vol. 60, No. 5, 1966, p. 141–6; G. H. Stockton, 'Effectiveness of Programmed Learning in Braille Instruction for the Adult Blind', doctoral dissertation, University of Wisconsin, 1965.

32. C. J. Kederis, C. Y. Nolan and J. E. Morris, 'The Use of Controlled Exposure Devices to Increase Braille Reading Rates', *International Journal for the Education of the Blind,* Vol. 16, 1867, p. 97–105.

33. Nolan and Kederis, op. cit., p. 15.

34. E. Foulke, *Report of the Perceptual Alternatives Laboratory for the Period 1 July 1973–30 June 1974,* p. 27, Louisville, Ky., Perceptual Alternatives Laboratory of the University of Louisville.

35. Kirman, op. cit.

36. V. McBride, 'Explorations in Rapid Reading in Braille', *New Outlook for the Blind,* Vol. 68, January 1974, p. 8–12.

37. Ibid, p. 10–11.

38. M. Olson, S. Harlow and J. Williams, 'Rapid Reading in Braille and Large Print: An Examination of McBride's Procedures', *New Outlook for the Blind,* Vol. 69, No. 9, November 1975, p. 392–5.

39. G. Spache, *Diagnostic Reading Scales,* Monterey, Calif., CTB/McGraw-Hill, 1963.

40. Olson, Harlow and Williams, op. cit.

41. McBride, op. cit., p. 12.

42. J. Lorimer, *The Limitations of Braille as a Medium for Communication and the Possibility of Improving Reading Standards,* p. 5, Birmingham, Research Centre for the Education of the Visually Handicapped, University of Birmingham, April 1978.

43. Ibid., p. 4–5.

44. See Gray and Todd, op. cit., p. 75.

45. M. J. Tobin, *Programmed Instruction and Braille Learning,* Birmingham, Research Centre for the Education of the Visually Handicapped, University of Birmingham, 1971.

46. M. J. C. Mommers, 'Some Factors Related to Braille Reading by Blind Children in Elementary Schools', unpublished report, Institute for Educational Sciences, Katholieke Universiteit, Erasmuslaan 40, Nijmegen.

47. Nolan and Kederis, op. cit., p. 9.

48. Lorimer, op. cit.

49. C. Y. Nolan and J. E. Morris, 'Development and Validation of the Roughness Discrimination Test', *International Journal for the Education of the Blind,* Vol. 15, 1965, p. 1–6.

50. Tobin, op. cit.

51. Mommers, op. cit.

52. See for example: R. Brown, 'Psychology and Reading', in H. Levin and J. P. Williams (eds.), *Basic Studies on Reading,* p. 164–87, New York, N.Y., Basic Books Inc., 1970; J. A. Fodor and M. Garret, 'Some Syntactic Determinants of Sentential Complexity', *Perception and Psychophysics,* Vol. 2, 1967, p. 289–96.

53. M. J. Tobin, *The Vocabulary of the Young Blind School Child,* Liverpool, Lancs., College of Teachers of the Blind, 1972.

54. Tobin, *Programmed Instruction...,* op. cit.

55. J. S. Chall, *Learning to Read: The Great Debate,* p. 307, New York, N.Y., McGraw-Hill, 1967.

56. Lowenfeld et al., op. cit., p. 46–7.

57. Nolan and Kederis, op. cit.

58. Ibid.

59. N. Norris, *Aims and Methods in the Teaching of English to the Visually Handicapped,* Birmingham, Research Centre for the Education of the Visually Handicapped, University of Birmingham, 1972.

60. Tobin, *Programmed Instruction...,* op. cit., p. 1.

61. Ibid, p. 110.

62. E. J. Rex, 'A Study of the Basal Readers and Experimental Supplementary Instructional Materials for Teaching Primary Reading in Braille. Part. I: An Analysis of Braille Features in Basal Readers',

Education of the Visually Handicapped, Vol. 2, No. 4, December 1970; 'Part II: Instructional Material for Teaching Reading in Braille', *Education of The Visually Handicapped*, Vol. 3, No. 1, March 1971.

63. *The Family Books; The Handbook to the Reading Schemes*, prepared by the College of Teachers of the Blind, Royal School for the Blind, Church Road North, Liverpool L15 6TQ, 1974.

64. M. J. Tobin, *A Study of the Vocabulary of the Young Blind School Child*, Birmingham, Research Centre for Education of the Visually Handicapped, University of Birmingham, 1971.

65. Personal communication from B. Hechle, Hon. Registrar, College of Teachers of the Blind, 27 November 1978.

66. *Proposal for Project 'Development of a Beginning Braille Reading Series'*, p. 2, 1977 (submitted by American Printing House for the Blind, Louisville, Ky.).

67. S. S. Mangold, 'The Effects of a Developmental Teaching Approach of Tactile Perception and Braille Letter Recognition Based on a Model of Precision Teaching', p. 259 (Ph. D. Thesis, University of California in Berkeley, Calif., 1977); See also, S. S. Mangold, 'Tactile Perception and Braille Letter Recognition: Effects of Developmental Teaching', *Journal of Visual Impairment and Blindness*, Vol. 72, No. 7, September 1978, p. 259-66.

68. The inkprint teacher's manual and two volumes of students' worksheets may be obtained by contacting Exception Teaching Aids, 20102 Woodbine Avenue, Castro Valley, CA 94546 (United States).

69. Mangold, op. cit., p. 264–5.

Chapter 6

Braille research

Introduction

Braille research is an activity which has grown and come to dominate meetings, both national and international, since the 1960s. There was, of course, a considerable amount of research carried out earlier. The factor, however, which differentiates between research during the past twenty years or so and that carried out earlier is 'organization'; that is, the establishment of research registers and research centres especially for the visually handicapped, and generally a considerable exchange of ideas and co-operation between institutes and organizations working in the field of blindness.

One landmark for the beginning of this development can be taken as the International Congress on Technology and Blindness (New York, 1962).[1] The congress was planned from within a project initiated in 1960 called 'An International Survey of Technical Devices Designed for the Education, Rehabilitation and Personal Aid of Blind Persons', which was undertaken by the American Foundation for the Blind. Out of this project, the International Research Information Service (IRIS) was created. This service took over the publication of the *AFB Research Bulletin* (which it issued at fairly regular intervals up to 1975), produced a research register and a catalogue of aids and appliances, and organized a series of international meetings.

Thus, during the 1960s the AFB was the focus for information on research activities. These pioneering developments stimulated the beginning of more organized research in Europe. A number of research centres was established, in the Federal Republic of Germany, Sweden and the United Kingdom during the 1960s and early 1970s. Recently the Warwick Research Unit for the Blind (United Kingdom), together with AFB, has begun to issue a regular newsletter on Braille research and has produced an *International Register of Research on Blindness and Visual Impairment* which covers information about projects, organizations, and sources of information on a world-wide basis.

A considerable amount of this research activity has been concentrated on Braille.

Studies on both technological and psychological/educational aspects have been undertaken.

One factor underlying this organization of research is that researchers, especially those within officially recognized research centres, have taken over much of the initiative for change in this area. Earlier, practically all change had come from within organizations of and for the blind. These organizations had, and have, a considerable responsibility to a wide range of people with a wide range of needs and abilities. If 'science and technology' is allowed to dominate totally, there is always a danger of just those scientifically and technologically 'interesting' areas being considered. The result of this can be that only a small number of the visually handicapped population benefit.

This aspect is particularly relevant to research on communication, which, of course, includes Braille. During recent years there has been a hectic development of information and communication technology generally. Not only has this resulted in more widespread and earier possibilities for communication, but it has also created the need to have efficient access to increasing amounts of information as well as the ability to process such information. This has created a situation where each new technical advance for the visually handicapped has been accompanied by new demands on them in terms of access to and processing of more information just to be able to keep up.

This situation has naturally created increasing concentration on research and development. In addition, however, it has also widened the gap between the able and the less able among the visually handicapped population. This can be seen, for example, between the facilities currently available to blind computer programmers and those available to the deaf-blind. Another example of this trend can be seen in the increasing discrepancy between facilities available in developed countries and those available in less technologically advanced nations.

In this chapter a brief overview will be given of the recent trends in reseach activities since the early 1960s. During this time there have been two major areas of research and development—educational/psychological and technological. The present needs and problems of these two areas will be discussed separately. Finally, some additional problems related to Braille will be discussed from the viewpoint of research.

Recent trends in research

The 1960s was a decade of 'technological boom' and technology relating to Braille production, storage and presentation was no exception to this trend. It took, however, the best part of the decade before the real benefits of these developments really began to be realized. As Clark wrote in 1975: 'No longer does one have occasion to complain, as we did not too many years ago, of the "vast wasteland" of sensory aids that were technologically sophisticated but ill-suited to the uses that humans put them to.'[2]

Most of the more obvious achievements of research, such as the development of Braille translation programmes and our increased understanding of the Braille reading process, are reviewed in the appropriate chapters of this book. However, other important developments, perhaps of a less direct nature, have also occurred, for example, the establishment of a number of companies, which have taken over many of the problems of developing and distributing Braille technology. Most of these companies are in the United Sates (see Appendix B), to a certain extent because their internal market is often sufficient to begin a reasonable serial production before going into the rather more expensive and complicated business of export. These companies now play a significant part in ensuring the continuing development of application-orientated equipment, which, for their own survival, must be well-designed, reliable and well-suited to immediate or short-term future needs. This, in turn, implies keeping a close contact with users and their organizations. However, the general problem of transfer of developments carried out in universities or research institutes is still largely unsolved where there are no direct commercial interests.

Another important development during the 1960s and 1970s has been that of documentation and information dissemination. Since the development of IRIS, a number of sources of information have become established (see Appendix C for details of these). The contribution and importance of information services is well summarized by Clark:

For some time, it appeared as if information control was a convenience for the researcher and for the practitioner; we simply needed to know who was doing what so that we could minimise effort and keep total costs of research and translation into practice as low as practicable. These motivations still obtain, of course, but gradually the awareness has grown that without some way to keep track of what has been done, what is being done, and what thinking informs the plan to put into practice what has been learned, we shall compound the mistakes of inept translation into practice, inappropriate inference from investigations, and the creation of a false sense of confidence in our understanding, that have obtained in the past. To the degree that we gain skill in undertaking research—both 'basic' and 'applied'—then to the same degree do our needs for appropriate information control grow and deepen. I think there is a growing understanding that the help of professionals is needed here, whether or not we use machine-aided techniques of information control; and this is a hopeful development, since it will, at the same time, facilitate cooperation among documentation research centres in several parts of the world.[3]

Another aspect of the increased organization of information and documentation has been the growth of a number of 'research centres'. The activities of these centres cover a wide range of studies in the area of visual handicap, and many have projects relating specifically to Braille.

Needs and problems
in educational/psychological research on Braille

A great deal of research has been carried out on Braille reading during the last two decades and our knowledge of the Braille reading process is now relatively sophisticated. This knowledge of Braille reading tends, however, to be kept within the academic circles and there seems a serious lack of studies on how best to apply and test the results of academic research. There are two main aspects: (i) those relating to the Braille code and (ii) those relating to teaching.

Research on Braille code

Research seems to indicate fairly clearly that the complexity of highly contracted Braille code systems is largely responsible for the difficulties which both children and adults have in learning Braille. Many countries, however, continue to support the idea of highly contracted Braille systems, which only a small, educated élite can use.

Teaching Braille reading

As indicated by Chapter 5, the literature on teaching Braille reading is considerable. The number of children and adults successfully learning to read Braille is, however, unacceptably low and a major reason for this is the lack of adequate facilities for teaching it. To some extent research can aid this situation by helping to design appropriate beginning reading materials. However, most reviews of reading research conclude that where a teacher is having success with a particular approach, he or she should continue to follow that approach no matter what the results of reading research might suggest.

Following this through, it would seem preferable to concentrate on providing teachers with information which they can use in whatever method they have success with, rather than trying to isolate any one particular method or technique as being 'the best'. Two factors associated with the teaching of Braille reinforce this approach for Braille teachers. First, in the case of contracted Braille, special problems are created by the use of contractions and no special 'method' for teaching can substitute for a thorough knowledge of the effects these contractions have on reading and learning to read. This information research can now begin to provide. Secondly, Braille teaching is often carried out on an individual basis. Even where classes of blind children are taught, the range of ability is very large among these children, thus often demanding an individualized approach to teaching.

It is often inappropriate, therefore, to introduce methods or techniques of teaching that have been developed and tested in class situations. The teacher of Braille reading should be in a position to be able to assess each child as to his or her special weakness or ability, and to provide the appropriate level of teaching to each child.

This assumes, of course, that the teaching of Braille reading is regarded as a specialist subject requiring specially trained teachers and, furthermore, that diagnostic tests and beginning reading material are developed so that there is always sufficient good material at hand for teachers. The situation regarding teaching Braille to adults also deserves special attention. The existence of well-designed courses and materials for teaching braille to the newly blind is crucial if these people are to achieve any success in learning Braille. The situation of the adult is totally different to that of the child. The adult must learn again a skill—reading—which earlier he had already possessed. This involves a different approach to that taken for children who are learning to read for the first time. Also, adults require material whose contents are appropriate to their level of maturity; otherwise there will be little possibility to generate interest in the material.

There is, therefore, a real need for improvement in Braille teaching facilities, and this will depend to some extent on appropriate research being carried out. The training of teachers in sufficient quantity and quality to carry out the teaching will be critical. In this, research perhaps plays a rather lesser role.

Needs and problems in technological research and development

Clark emphasizes the danger of a too narrow approach to the research and development process:

There is something almost mystical about the search for 'the' solution to the problem of transducing visual information for those not having vision into other sensory forms (tactile, auditory and so on). And even highly experimental inquiries, like that of the introduction of electrical signals directly into the occipital cortex, have been seized upon both as 'the' solution to the problem of blindness, and as a reason for blunting the development of more mundane solutions to the several problems of interacting with the world that the blind and severely visually impaired persons face.[4]

The need to keep research and development going on a broad but co-ordinated front is particularly important when considering Braille. There is also 'something almost mystical' about Braille in many people's minds, who, as a result fail to see the problems of Braille provision in the wider context of developing a *range* of 'communication facilities' for the visually handicapped. Braille is, after all, a medium that will always be used by only a minority of the visually handicapped.

To say this, however, is not to deflate the importance of Braille as a communication medium; communication media should not be considered as 'competing' with each other. Braille is the superior medium for *some* people in *some* situations. The needs of these people in these situations should be the starting point for the research and development of Braille provision.

With the increasing penetration of technology and its effects, good and bad, into everybody's lives, the need for evaluation is crucial. This applies to Braille technology as much as to any other area.

Approaches to evaluation

There are a large number of approaches to the problem of evaluating the worth of any particular technological development. Some of these, together with the central questions they attempt to answer, are given in Table 1.

Table 1. Some different approaches to technology evaluation [5]

Type of study	Central questions to be answered
Feasibility	Is it a workable and safe design? Can it be done/developed with available resources and techniques? What will it cost?
Market research	Who will use it? Who will pay for it? What is the demand? Can demand be influenced?
Cost-benefit [1]	What are the monetary costs? What are the monetary benefits? What is the net difference between costs and benefits? What is the benefit-to-cost ratio? Which alternative will maximize the net value of benefits?
Cost-effectiveness	What are the costs of alternative ways of obtaining a particular set of outcomes (e.g. improved Braille provision)? Which alternative will maximize the desired outcomes for any particular level of resources
Technology assessment	What is the state-of-the-art of the technology? Are there better alternatives to achieve the objective? What are its potential second or higher order impacts and consequences? How will these impacts and consequences interact with each other? Who are the parties-at-interest and how will they be affected? Who are the decision-makers and what is the potential for the consumers to influence the outcome?

1. Exceptionally, cost-benefit studies can include non-monetary values.

Table 1 shows a considerable range of sophistication in the approach taken to evaluation. The most straightforward is the feasibility study, which asks simply —'Does the equipment perform the function we want it to?' and 'Can we afford it?'. It doesn't ask whether that particular 'function' needs to be carried out, or, at least, whether it should have priority; neither does it ask whether, as a result of carrying out this 'function', other aspects in the overall situation may get worse, resulting in an overall poorer service. The questions asked, on the other hand, by the more sophisticated, technology assessment are addressed to these wider and deeper issues.

We can, by way of example, consider the situation of a country wanting to introduce a computerized Braille production system. Such an innovation often creates a need for changes in the Braille code in order that the translation programme can be made acceptably efficient, as in the Federal Republic of Germany and Denmark, for example. How will the Braille code be changed? Will 'translatability' be the dominating influence? If so, there is a risk that this may have adverse effects on the readability or may be considered unacceptable by a significant number of readers. This, in turn, may reduce demand and thereby undermine the need for the introduction of any new Braille production technology. If, on the other hand, research facilities can be utilized to develop a new code where readability and acceptability play a significant role in its development, then reading may be stimulated by the improved service possible with the new technology. This, in turn, may require the capacity estimates of the new system to be revised upwards. In this latter case, additional factors must be considered. For example, are Braille teaching facilities in schools and rehabilitation centres adequate to take advantage of this potential increase in demand?

To take another example, again involving a large-scale investment in Braille production facilities; will this large-scale investment in Braille technology make it more difficult to obtain investment capital for equipment to produce talking-books, large-print or sensory-aids for reading? If so, the overall consequence for information provision for the visually handicapped population may end up being poorer, owing to the far greater number of potential users of talking books and large-print. The opposite may also result in undesired consequences. That is, if large investment is made in talking-book and large-print production, this may have adverse affects on the possibility for developing Braille facilities, thereby sacrificing the needs of the few, which may be important and inappropriate to produce in another media, such as study material or material needed for work, to the needs of the many.

The question of who are the decision-makers is also an important one. For example, the development of 'paperless' Braille machines (see Appendix E) permits printing houses to rationalize their distribution systems by eliminating, or at least heavily reducing, their need to emboss books. Cassettes, encoded in Braille, may be sent out instead so that readers read the 'book' via their Braille displays. What influence will those people preferring the traditional-format book have in deciding whether this rationalization is carried through?

Any evaluation of a new technological development should involve, then, far more than just whether the equipment functions reliably and whether it's worth its price. Technological innovation has consequences far beyond the immediate technical rationalizations which it may permit. Evaluation should, therefore, also attempt to predict and to analyse these wider consequences of the innovation. This calls for the development of better and more sophisticated resources in the field of research utilization and evaluation. The people, or preferably, groups of people should be closely in tune with both the technological developments taking place and the realities, in this particular context, regarding provision of information for the visually handicapped.

Other areas requiring more research

Design and editing of Braille material

This is an area which has received scant attention from research. A certain amount of research has been carried out in this area relating to spoken material[6] and to illustrative material and maps in relief form.[7] Little, however, has been directed towards the problems of editing material and its layout so as to optimize its readability by Braille readers.

Some questions immediately spring to mind. How important are the various type fonts, sizes of type, etc., commonly used in print texts for facilitating the ease with which readers can structure the text; to what extent should these print techniques be included in the Braille translation and what is the most effective way of achieving this? What is the most effective form for setting out tabular information in Braille? What is the most effective form for setting out mathematical, scientific, music texts, i.e. can the informational and spatial structuring of the various code systems be evaluated in terms of readability, effective layout, ease of learning, etc. How effective are relief figures in Braille books, and under what circumstances; can general principles be generated for helping to decide whether a figure should be produced in relief, described in the text, or left out?

A particularly important research need in this area has been created by the development of 'paperless' Braille equipment (see Appendix E). For example, what is the effect on reading of only having a single line of characters available at any one time? What is the optimum number of characters in such a display line? Is there a need to have special 'format characters' such as 'end of paragraph', 'rubric', etc., in order to aid the reading process? If so, what should these 'format characters' be and how could they be displayed? Apropos research on 'paperless' Braille equipment, there is a need for a general and independent ergonomic investigation focusing on appropriateness in different situations, as an aid to studying, as an aid at work, as a 'reading machine', etc.

Code systems

In 1976 Douce and Tobin published a paper calling for a detailed and thorough study of the Standard English Braille code system.[8] In that paper they outlined the following programme of work:

(i) A representative selection of textual material comprising sections of novels, textbooks, short documents and correspondence will be assembled. An analysis similar to that reported by Lockhead and Lorimer will be undertaken;[9] the significant differences being that the analysis will be done from data in computer-readable form, and will consider a larger amount of material.
(ii) A wide range of users and experts will be consulted for suggested revision.
(iii) A statistical study will be undertaken on the effects of the proposed revisions, to assess their significance with regard to potential reduction in the number of rules and saving space.

(iv) Revisions showing promise will be evaluated in carefully designed experiments to test their effects on learning time, reading speed and acceptability.

(v) Feedback from these experiments will be used to improve the proposals and refine the experiments, hopefully leading to definitive results backed by scientific evidence supporting, or refuting, the case for modifying Grade 2 Braille.[10]

This project has now been funded and is under way, with the Research Centre for the Education of the Visually Handicapped (see Appendix D 6) carrying out the educational research, and the Warwick Research Unit for the Blind (see Appendix D 9) the engineering and analytic studies.

Similar interest in revising the Braille code has also developed in the United States, especially on the occasion of the workshop on 'Computerized Braille' held in 1976 in New York.[11] In October 1978 a seminar was held in New York to plan an analogous project to the English one, i.e. Douce and Tobin's project, for the United States, to be co-ordinated as far as possible with the English project so that, hopefully, the English and American code systems will have a better chance to achieve some degree of standardization. Other English-speaking countries will also be consulted during the course of these projects.

These projects represent an important step towards creating a methodology for investigating Braille code systems and a considerable bank of basic data relating to readability of Braille characters, not least because the starting points of both projects are the ease of learning and reading Braille rather than the ease of machine translation.

Many countries currently use as many contractions as the English system, and some significantly more, e.g. French, Spanish, Portuguese. These English/American projects should motivate other countries to critically examine their own Braille codes with a view to simplification regarding ease of learning and reading, and of extending provision, thereby, to a wider group of people.

Braille provision for the deaf-blind

As mentioned in the introduction to this chapter, technological developments, especially in the area of communication have, in certain cases, served to widen the gap between the able and the less able within the handicapped population. One example of this is the deaf-blind.

Some developments have made significant contributions to helping the deaf-blind communicate with their fellow human beings. For example, equipment which can be interfaced to a telephone and which enables a deaf-blind person, via a keyboard and a Braille, or other appropriate, display, to use, in a limited way, the telephone. In general, however, the main problems for this group do not always lie so much with technological developments as with editing and presentation of the material.

People who have a severe hearing loss from birth, or soon after, often have impaired language development, also. This, coupled with the handicap of blindness, can, although not, of course, necessarily, pose severe difficulties for that person to develop his/her full potential. An ordinary Braille book or magazine can, therefore, contain many concepts and words which many among the deaf-blind do not understand.

Braille provision for the deaf-blind can, therefore, involve more than just the technical production of the material. It can involve rewriting texts in a simpler form—using short sentences, straightforward grammatical structures, commonly occurring words, etc. The use of such techniques in the design of Braille material for the deaf-blind deserves a significant research effort. Such a research effort also implies that thorough investigations of both abilities and needs of the deaf-blind are also carried out.

Notes

1. L. L. Clark, *Proceedings of the International Congress on Technology and Blindness*, Vols. I, II and III, New York, N.Y.. American Foundation for the Blind, 1963.
2. L.L. Clark, 'Research Resource Needs for the Future', *New Outlook for the Blind*, Vol. 69, No. 2, February 1975, p. 49–61.
3. Ibid., p. 50–2.
4. Ibid., p. 51.
5. Based on table given in S.R. Artstein, 'Technology Assessment: Opportunities and Obstacles', *IEEE Transactions on Systems, Man and Cybernetics*, Vol. SMC-7, No. 8, August 1977, p. 576.
6. N. Trowald, *Fran text till tal* [From Printed Text to Talking Book], Stockholm, Liber Utbildnings-förlaget, 1978 (FOU report 33).
7. See, for example, C. Y. Nolan, *Facilitating the Education of the Visually Handicapped through Research in Communications* Part III: *Facilitating Tactile Map Reading; Final Report,* 1976 (Grant No. OEG-0-73-0642, US Department of Health, Education and Welfare, Office of Education).
8. J.L. Douce and M.L. Tobin, 'Discussion Paper on the Desirability of a Joint Research Project on the Braille Code, Extending the Use of Braille, and the Improvement of Reading Skills', *Braille Automation Newsletter,* February 1976, p. 5–7.
9. H.M. Lockhead and J. Lorimer, *Report of the Survey of the Frequency of all the Contractions of Standard English Braille Grade 2,* Edinburgh, Scottish Braille Press, Craigmiller Park, 1954.
10. Douce and Tobin, op. cit., p. 7.
11. R. A. J. Gildea and M. Berkowitz, 'Computerized Braille', *Proceedings of a Workshop on Compliance of Computer Programs with English Braille, American Edition, New York City, 7–8 June 1976* (ACM and AFB 1977).

Appendices

Appendix A

Presses and Braille libraries

1. *Algeria*   Organisation Nationale des Aveugles Algériens
     4 Bd Mohamed
     Khemisti
     Algiers

Carry out Braille production and have Braille library.

2. *Argentina*   Biblioteca Argentina para Ciegos
     Lezica 3909
     esq Medrano
     Buenos Aires

Braille library — 6,936 titles of which 25 per cent are for children under 12 and 75 per cent for adolescents and adults. There are about 2,500 textbooks for university and secondary school students. Loans are made to anyone who requests them.

     Institute Hellen Keller para Ciegos
     Ave. Velez Sarsfield 2.100
     Cordoba

Braille library — 1,600 titles of which 10 per cent are for children and remainder for adolescents and adults. There are about 45 textbooks for secondary school and university students. Loans are made to other Spanish-speaking countries.

3. *Australia*   Royal Blind Society of New South Wales
     Box 176
     P.O. Burwood
     New South Wales 2134

Braille library — 4,600 titles of which 6.5 per cent are for children under 12 and the remainder for adolscents and adults. There are about 20 textbooks for secondary school and university students. Loans are made without any special conditions.

     Braille Library of Victoria
     31-51 Commercial Road
     South Yarra
     Victoria

Free lending library for the blind providing free tuition in Braille for its readers.

Royal Victorian Institute for the Blind
557 St Kilda Road
Melbourne
Victoria 3004

Small-scale thermoform duplication of texts requested and selected by teachers at the institute. Willing to loan books, at borrower's expense, if copies exist.

Royal New South Wales Institute for Deaf and
Blind Children
111-115 Chandos Street
St Leonards
Sydney
New South Wales

First computerized Braille system in Australia. Currently operating with two input stations producing about 2,000 original Braille pages per month (November 1978).

4. *Austria*   Leihbücherei, Druckerei und Lehrmittelverlag des
Bundes-Blindenerziehungs-Institutes
A-1020 Vienna 11
Wittelsbachstrasse 5

Braille printing house with computer-aided facilities and Braille library.

5. *Bangladesh*   Bangladesh National Society for the Blind
12 Felder Street
Wari
Dacca 3

Braille library established in February 1977.

6. *Belgium*   Licht en Liefde voor onze Blinden
Jerusalemstraat 19
B-8000
Brugge

Braille library—2,197 titles of wich 17 per cent are for children under 12 and the remainder for adolescents and adults. There are about 52 textbooks for secondary school and university students. Willing to loan books to other countries without any special conditions.

Other Braille libraries include:

Ligue Braille
57 rue d'Angleterre
B-1060 Brussels

Œuvre Nationale des Aveugles
Avenue Dailly 90-92
B-1030 Brussels

7. *Brazil*   Fundacão Para o Livro do Cego no Brasil
Rua Dr Diogo de Faria 558
Caixo Postal 20384
São Paulo

Braille book production. Braille correspondence course.

8. *Canada*   Canadian National Institute for the Blind
1929 Bayview Avenue
Toronto
Ontario M4G 3E8

Computerized Braille production facilities using system partly purchased from Duxbury Systems Inc. (see Appendix B 8(c) (ii)). Triformation LED-120 printers (see Appendix B (b) (i)). Braille library—7,120 titles of which 12 per cent are for children under 12. There are about 1,380 textbooks for secondary school and university students. Willing to loan to other countries provided request comes from recognized official agency for the blind.

9. *Czechoslovakia* Svaz invalidu, federlni vybor
Karlinske namesti 12
186 03 Praha
8-Karlin

Braille production.

10. *Denmark* State Library and Printing House for the Blind
Rönnegade 1
2100 Copenhagen Ø

Braille production partly by computerized translation of texts. Texts keypunched and translated using commercial service bureaux. IBM 1403 used for Braille output. Braille library — 3,000 titles of which 95 per cent are for adolescents and adults. Willing to loan books without any special conditions.

11. *Finland* Sokeain Keskusliitto r.y.
Makelankatu 52
00510 Helsinki 51

Braille printing house and Braille library. At the end of 1973 the library had 4,947 titles and 345 new titles were produced in 1973. Approximately half the books are of specialized material.

12. *France* Association Valentin Haüy
5-9 rue Duroc
75007 Paris

The association has two printing houses; one in Paris and the other in Lyon. The main Braille library is in Paris, with regional branches in Lyon, Marseilles, Nice and Rennes. The Paris and Lyon printing houses produce about 120,000 volumes of stereotype Braille each year. The Paris library, which co-ordinates the work of some 700 home-working transcribers, produces about 500–600 titles each year.

Centre TOBIA (see Appendix D 7)

Created in 1977, this centre has now produced 23,000 Braille pages — school books, novels, special documents, bank statements etc. — using their computer-aided production facilities.
A number of specialist societies exist in France which produce Braille, e.g. Le Livre de l'Aveugle (9 rue Duroc, 75007 Paris), an association mainly for war-blinded, provides books for academic and profession purposes. Their stock is about 100,000 volumes which consist mainly of specialist academic material.

13. *German Democratic Republic* Deutsche Zentralbücherei für Blinde
Gustav-Adolf Strasse 7
DDR 701 Leipzig

Braille library — 6,900 titles of which 90 per cent are for adolescents and adults. There are 30 textbooks for secondary school students. Willing to loan books to any other country without special conditions.

14. *Federal Republic of Germany* Deutsche Blindenstudienanstalt
Am Schlag 8
D-3550 Marburg
(Lahn)

Verein zur Förderung der Blindenbildung e.
3 Hannover 71
Bleekstrasse 26

These are the two main printing houses. The former tends to concentrate on book production — school books, law, scientific and the specialist books — whereas the latter tends to concentrate on magazine production. In addition to Blindenstudienanstalt, there are nine other libraries for the blind which altogether stock 10,000 titles. The number of Braille books in the German University Library for the Blind (at Blindenstudienanstalt) stands at about 52,000.

15. *Guatemala*   Comite Nacional Pro-Ciegos Y Sordomudoa
                  4a Avenida 2-28
                  Zona 1

Centralized circulating Braille library.

16. *Hong Kong*   The Special Education Section
                  Education Department
                  Lee Gardens, Hyson Avenue

                  Hong Kong Society for the Blind
                  33 Grandville Road
                  Kowloon

Both have thermoform Braille reproduction facilities. About 20 English and 4 Cantonese titles are produced per year, these being mainly textbooks. There is no central library for all books but the main library is at the Hong Kong Society for the Blind. They have about 800 titles, all of which are for adolescents and adults. There are about 300 textbooks available for secondary school and university students. These are not loaned to other countries.

17. *Hungary*   Association of Blind and Visually Handicapped
                Majus 1-ut 47
                H-1146 Budapest XIV

Braille printing house and library. Library has 1,159 titles of which 167 are for children under 12, leaving 275 for adolescents and 737 for adults. There are also 7 textbooks for students at the Faculty of Law. Willing to loan books to other countries without any special conditions. There is also a library at the school for the blind which has 921 titles.

18. *India*   There are four Braille printing houses in India:
              National Association for the Blind Regional Braille
                  Press
              Jehangir Wadia Building
              51 Mahatma Gandhi Road
              Bombay 400 03

              Regional Braille Press
              c/o Government School for the Blind
              Poonamalee
              Madras
              Tasmil Nadu

              Regional Braille Press
              c/o National School for the Blind
              Rajpur Road
              Bodyguard Lane
              Dehra Dun
              Uttar Pradesh
              (this press is owned and operated by the
                  Government of India)

              Regional Braille Press
              c/o Blind Boys Academy
              Narendrapur
              24 Parganas
              West Bengal

These four presses each serve an area of India. The large number of officially recognized languages is a problem—the NAB produces Braille material in English, Marathi, Gujarati and Hindi. Textbooks are produced mainly. Libraries are usually managed by voluntary organization, for example, the Blind Men's Associations of Bombay and Ahmedabad have their own libraries. The Delhi Public Library, 425 Lakshmibai, Nagar, New Delhi 5, has a Braille section. These libraries will loan books to other countries.

19. *Indonesia*   Indonesian Braille Printing and Publishing Institute
Jl. Pajajaran 52
Bandung

Mostly textbooks are produced. Braille is also produced in at least seven other places, mainly on a 'service' basis. There are four Braille libraries including one at the above address.

20. *Iran*   National Organisation for the Welfare of the
Iranian Blind
Avenue France
38 Marjan Street
Tehran

Braille printing house.

21. *Israel*   Jewish Institute for the Blind—Jerusalem
P.O. Box 925
Kiryat Moshe
91000 Jerusalem

Braille printing house.

22. *Italy*   Biblioteca Italiana per Ciechi 'Regina Margherita'
Villa Reale
20052 Monza

Braille library—5,197 titles of which 94 per cent are for adolescents and adults. There are 472 textbooks for secondary school and university students. Willing to loan books to other countries without special conditions.

23. *Japan*   Nippon Tenji Toshokan
1-23-4 Takadano-baba
Shinjuku-ku
Tokyo

Braille press and library intended mainly for adults; willing to loan Braille books to other countries. They have 75,000 Braille volumes.

Nippon Lighthouse Welfare Center for the Blind
4-37 Naka 2-chome
Imazu
Tsurumi-ku
Osaka City 538

Braille printing-press and library. In addition, the following libraries exist:
Niigata Tenju Toshokan
1-57-1 Kawagishi-cho
Niigata-shi

Stock of 17,500 Braille books of standard recreation literature.

Shigaken Tenji Toshokan
800 Nishi-Ima-cho
Hikone-shi
Shiga-ken

Stock of 7,000 Braille books.

Iwate-ken Tenji Toshokan
Kitayama
Morioka-shi
Iwate-ken

Approximately 9,000 Braille books of which 4,000 are recreation literature.

Okayama-ken Tenji Toshokan
799 Haraojima-Osunaba
Okayama-shi

Braille stock of 6,700 books of which 3,800 are recreational.

Kagoshima-ken Tenji Toshokan
28 Ono-cho
Kagoshima-shi

Stock of 7,000 Braille books of which 2,500 are recreational.

Ohita Tenji Toshokan
3-1-75 Kanaike
Ohita-shi

Nagoya-shi Chuoh Toshokan Tenji-Bunko
155-1-1 Tsurumai
Showaku
Nagoya-shi

Stock of 1,200 Braille books of which 800 are recreational.

Nagano-ken Ueda Tenji Toshokan
5-2-1 Zaimokucho
Uedashi
Nagano-ken

Stock of 9,000 Braille books which are nearly all recreational. They also have production facilities.

National Tokyo Center for the Visually
 Handicapped
2-34-18 Umezato
Suginami-ku
Tokyo

24. *Jordan*   National Library for the Blind
P.O. Box 27
Beit
Jala via Israel

25. *Malaysia*   Braille Library
Malaysian Association for the Blind
P.O. Box 687
Kuala Lumpur

There are 1,300 Braille titles of which nearly all are for adolescents and adults. There are about 100 textbooks for secondary school and university students. Willing to loan books to Singapore and Indonesia via agency of/for the blind.

26. *Mexico*   Comite International Pro Ciegos
Mariano Azuela 218
Mexico 4 D.F.

Braille publishing and library.

27. *Netherlands*   Dutch Library for the Blind
Zilhtenburglaan 260
The Hague

This is the main source of Braille and the major library. Computerized Braille production and book loaning systems.

Stichting Coördinatie-centrum
Amstel 177
1018 ES Amsterdam

No production or library facilities but acts in organizational capacity on behalf of other libraries for the blind. Mainly concerned with more specialized Braille needs.

Blindenbibliotheek 'Le Sage Ten Broek'
Panovenlaan 1
Nijmegen

Produces most of the books for schools.

Royal Institute for the Blind
Amersfoortsestraatweg 180
Huizen/post Bussum

Produces Braille books for its own needs.

Christelijke Blindenbibliotheek
Postbox 131
Putterweg
140 Ermelo

Production and lending of Braille books.

Vereniging Het Nederlandsche Blindenwezen
Kipstraak 54
Rotterdam – 3001

Braille production facilities.

28. *New Zealand*   Royal New Zealand Foundation for the Blind
Private Bag
Newmarket
Auckland 1

Production of Braille books.

29. *Norway*   Norges Blindeforbunds
Trykkeri
Rosenkrantzgaten 3
N-5000 Bergen

Norway's printing house for the blind.

Norges Blindeforbund

Has three regional libraries:

Norges Blindeforbund
Ovre Mollenberggaten 76
N-7000 Trondheim

Norges Blindeforbund
Rosenkrantzgaten 3
N-5000 Bergen

Norges Blindeforbund
Sporveisgaten 10
N Oslo 3.

Braille stocks include 1,500 titles of which 90 per cent are for adults.

30. *Pakistan* Pakistan Association of the Blind
160 1st Floor
KMC Garden Market
Nishtar Road
Karachi-3

Braille transcription service and Braille libraries.

31. *Philippines* Philippine Printing House for the Blind
Department of Education and Culture
Arroceros Street
Manila

Philippine National School for the Blind Library
F. B. Harrison Street
Pasay City

Textbooks and supplementary books mostly for elementary and secondary level.

32. *Portugal* Centro Professional
Albuquerque e Castro
Rua do Instituto S. Manuel
Oporto
(Printing house for the blind)

There are two material centres providing Braille among other things for children in integrated education:

Centro de Producão de Material
Av. Almurante
Reis 133-4 E
1100 Lisbon

(The address of the material centre in Oporto can be obtained from the above address.)

33. *Saudi Arabia*

Information about the Braille printing facilities can be obtained from:

Adbullah M. Al-Ghanim
Regional Bureau of the Middle East Committee
for the Welfare of the Blind
P.O. Box 3465
Riyadh

34. *Singapore* Singapore Association for the Blind
47 Toa Payoh
Rise
Singapore 11

National Library of Singapore
Stamford Road
Singapore 6

Braille library—398 titles of which approximately half are for children under 12.

35. *South Africa* School for the Blind
20 Adderley Street
Worcester
6850 Cape Province

Braille library—2,884 titles of which one-third are for school children and two-thirds are for adolescents and adults. There are approximately 100 titles for secondary school and university students.

South African Library for the Blind
P.O. Box 116
High Street
6140 Grahamstown

Braille library—5,548 titles of which most are for adolescents and adults; willing to loan to other countries through recognized agencies for the blind.

36. *Spain*   Organización Nacional de Ciegos de España
Jose Ortega y Gasset 18
Madrid 6

Braille printing house. This organization also has a Braille printing house in Barcelona.

Imprenta Braille
Pedro IV
78-84-1ᵉ
Barcelona 5

Biblioteca Central Braille
C/Prim 3
Madrid 4

Braille library—5,100 titles of which nearly all are for adolescents and adults. There are 652 titles for secondary school and university students; willing to loan Braille books to other countries not too distant, i.e. Europe and North Africa.

37. *Sweden*   Synskadades Riksförbund
Tal och Punkt
S-122 88 Enskede

Main printing house for the blind which utilizes computer-aided Braille production techniques (see Chapter 3).

Swedish Library for the Blind
S-122 88 Enskede

Braille library—4,400 titles of which most are for adolescents and adults. There are 250 titles for secondary school and university students.

Rikscentralen för pedagogiska hjälpmedel at
synskadade
Tomtebodavägen 11
171 64 Solna

Co-ordinating centre for materials, including Braille production for school children in integrated education.

38. *Switzerland*   Bibliothèque Braille Romande
34 Bourg-de-Four
1204 Geneva

Braille library—5,000 titles of which nearly all are for adolescents and adults. There are between 600 and 800 titles for secondary school and university students. Are willing to loan books within Europe only.

Leihbibliothek der Schweiz
Caritasaktion der Blinden
Leihbibliothek CAB
Blindenzentrum Landschlacht
8597 Landschlacht/TG

Braille library—1,100 titles. Willing to loan books to other German-speaking countries.

Biblioteca Braille per ciechi della Svizzera italiana
via S. Gottardo
6598 Tenero

Braille library—485 titles of which 90 per cent are for adolescents and adults. There are 20 titles for secondary school and university students.

Schweiz Blindenschriftbibliothek
Kreuzstrasse 68
8008 Zurich

Braille library—approximately 3,500 titles, excluding music scores, most of which are for adolescents and adults. They have 3,500 books for secondary school and university students, about 2,000 of which are scientific books of all categories.

39. *Taiwan*   Committee for the Blind of Taiwan
P.O. Box 10
Hsin Chuan
Taipei Hsien

Braille publishing.

40. *Thailand*

A Braille printing house was established in Thailand in 1979. Details from:

The Association of the Blind
420 Rajawiti Road
Bangkok 5

41. *Union of Soviet*   RSFSF Central Library for the Blind
Socialist Republics   29/33 Valovaja St.
Moscow M-54

Braille library—8,000 titles of which the majority are for adolescents and adults. There are 1,600 textbooks for secondary school and university students. Willing to loan books to other countries without special conditions.

42. *United Kingdom*   Royal National Institute for the Blind
Braille House
338-346 Goswell Road
London EC1N 7JE

Braille publishing and library. Braille printing house recently moved to new premises in conjunction with introduction of new computer-aided Braille production system (see Chapter 3). Braille library has about 10,000 titles all for adolescents and adults. A large proportion are for secondary school and university students. Willing to loan to other countries for a limited period.

Scottish Braille Press
Craigmullar Park
Edinburgh EH16 5NB
Scotland

Printing and publishing of Braille books and magazines for general distribution.

National Library for the Blind
Cromwell Road
Bredbury
Stockport SK6 2RF

Braille production in single or small numbers of copies using home-transcribers. Library has 40,000 titles of which 5,000 are for children under 12 and the rest for adolescents and adults. Willing to loan to other countries.

43. *United Republic*   Tanzania Braille Printing Press
of Tanzania   P.O. Box 3680
Dar-es-Salaam

44. *United States of*   American Printing House for the Blind, Inc.
America   1139 Frankfort Avenue
Louisville
Kentucky 40206

Manufacture of Braille books, music and magazines.

Braille Institute of America, Inc.
741 North Vermont Avenue
Los Angeles
California 90029

Publishes books and magazines in Braille.

Braille Circulating Library
2700 Stuart Avenue
Richmond
Virginia 23220

Clovernook Printing House for the Blind
7000 Hamilton Avenue
Cincinnati
Ohio 45231

Prints Braille books, magazines, catalogues and other publications for national organizations.

Jewish Braille Institute of America, Inc.
110 East 30th Street
New York
NY 10016

Will provide handcopy of any English book for anyone anywhere.

Library of Congress Division of the Blind and
Physically Handicapped
1291 Taylor Street N.W.
Washington, D.C. 20542

Conducts a free library service for the blind and physically handicapped.

Lutheran Braille Workers, Inc.
11735 Peach Tree Circle
Yucaipa
California 92399

An organization of volunteers producing Braille in thirty languages—mainly devotional and biblical.

National Braille Press, Inc.
88 St Stephens Street
Boston
Massachusetts 02115

Produces, on request, all kinds of material, including mathematics and music, in Braille.

National Braille Association
85 Godwin Avenue
Midland Park
New Jersey 07432

NBA Braille Book Bank provides thermoform copies of hand-transcribed texts to blind college and graduate students and professional people at below production cost.

Volunteer Services for the Blind, Inc.
919 Walnut Street
Philadelphia
Pennsylvania 19107

Provides material in Braille to students, business and professional people.

45. *Uruguay*   Fundación Braille del Uruguay
21 de Setiembre 2268
Montevideo

Publishes children's books in Braille.

46. *Yugoslavia*   Pokrajinska biblioteka
Saveza Slepih Vojvodine
21000 Novi Sad, Ul.
Svetogaro Miletica 28

Braille library—1,050 titles of which nearly 90 per cent are for adolescents and adults. There are 47 textbooks for secondary school and university students. Willing to loan books to other countries.

Republika biblioteka
Saveza slijepih Sobije 'Dr Milan Budumir'
11001 Beograd
Ustanicka 25/IV
Postannki fah 968

Braille library—1,242 titles, mainly for adolescents and adults. There are 56 textbooks for secondary school and university students. Willing to lend books to other countries.

Biblioteka Saveza slijepih Hrvatske
41000 Zagreb Ul.
Draskoviceva br. 80

Braille library—2,400 titles of which most are for adolescents and adults. There are 150 textbooks for secondary school and university students. Willing to lend books to other countries.
In addition, there are five other, smaller Braille libraries in Yugoslavia.

47. *Zimbabwe*   Jairos Jiri Association for Rehabilitation of the
Disabled and Blind
401 Southampton House
Main Street, 9th Avenue
Bulawayo

Council for the Blind
520 Portland House
Selborne Avenue
Salisbury

Appendix B

Manufacturers of equipment

1. *Braillewriters*

   (i)   *Stainsby Braillewriter*
                        Royal National Institute for
                            the Blind
                        224 Great Portland Street
                        London W1N 6AA
                        United Kingdom

   Downward Briallewriter available for writing interline or interpoint, or both. Ordinary or reversed keys.

   (ii)   *Blista (Marburg)*
         Braillewriter
                        Deutsche Blindenstudienanstalt
                        Am Schlag 8
                        Marburg (Lahn)
                        Federal Republic of Germany

   (iii)   *Perkins Brailler*
                        Howe Press of Perkins School for
                          the Blind
                        175 North Beacon Street
                        Watertown
                        Maryland 02172
                        United States

   Eletronically assisted model available from above address and:
                        The Swiss Central Union for the Blind
                        St Leonhard-Strasse 32
                        9000 St. Gallen
                        Switzerland

   (iv)   *IBM Braille electric*
         typewriter
                        IBM Corporation
                        Office Products Division
                        Parson's Pond Drive
                        Franklin Lakes
                        New Jersey 07417
                        United States

Braillewriters from the German Democratic Republic, Italy, Japan and the Republic of Korea are also listed in the *International Guide to Aids and Appliances for Blind and Visually Impaired Persons* (Appendix C).

2. *Braille duplicators*
    (i)   *Marburg Braille*   Deutsche Blindenstudienanstalt
            duplicator   Am Schlag 8
                                           Marburg (Lahn)
                                           Federal Republic of Germany

    (ii)   *Espinasse duplicator*   GIAA
                                           4 rue Bernard Mule
                                           31 Toulouse
                                           France

    (iii)   *Beatty's 'Kobraille'*   Professor K. O. Beatty
            process   Department of Chemical Engineering
                                           North Carolina State University
                                           Raleigh
                                           North Carolina 27607
                                           United States

    (iv)   *Vacuum-forming equipment*   American Thermoform Corporation
                                           8640 Slauson Avenue
                                           Pico Rivera
                                           CA 90660
                                           United States

                                           F. Kutschera & Co.
                                           3 Hannover
                                           Königsworther Strasse 7
                                           Federal Republic of Germany

            Plastic   American Thermoform Corporation
                                           (see above)
                                           A/S Helly-Hansen-Renolit
                                           P.O. Box 198
                                           N-1501
                                           Moss
                                           Norway

                                           Braas & Co. Gmbh
                                           Schildkröt-Kunststoffverke
                                           68 Mannheim 24
                                           Postfach 163/164
                                           Federal Republic of Germany

Plastic can also be obtained directly from RNIB, London (see 1 (i) above) and Deutsche Blindestudien-anstalt (see 2 (i) above).

    (v)   *Micronex Braille page*   Micronex Limited
            scanner   Harford Square
                                           Chew Magna
                                           Bristol BS18 8RA
                                           United Kingdom

(A Braille page reader has also been developed by Dr Osamu Sueda, Department of Biological Engineering, Faculty of Engineering Science, Osaka University, Toyonaka, Osaka 560, Japan.)

3. *Equipment for the Production of Braille*
    (a) *Stereotyping machines*
        (i)   *Marburg Braille*   Deutsche Blindenstudienanstalt
                stereotyper   (see 2 (i) above).
                Plate embossed horizontally. Electrically assisted. Keyboard for one or two-handed operation.

(ii)   *APH stereograph*   American Printing House for the Blind
       machine   1839 Frankfort Avenue
                                   Louisville
                                   KY 40206
                                   United States

Plate embossed vertically.

(iii) *Howe press stereograph*   Howe Press of Perkins School
       machine   for the Blind
                                   (see 1 (iii) above)

Plate embossed vertically.

(iv)   *Moy stereotyper*   Ernest F. Moy Ltd.
                                   116-134 Bayham Street
                                   London NW1 OBB
                                   United Kingdom

Stereotyping machines from Austria, France and Italy are listed in the *International Guide to Aids* (see Appendix C).

(b) *Braille encoding equipment*
    (i)   *Triformation*   3132 S.E. Jay Street
          Systems Inc.   Stuart
                                   Florida 33494
                                   United States

    (ii) SAGEM   Société d'Applications Générales
                                   d'Electricité et de Mécanique
                                   6 Avenue d'Iena
                                   75783 Paris Cedex 16
                                   France

Agents

Belgium	SAGEM B, 51 rue d'Arlon, 1040 Brussels
Israel	France Intertrade Sarl 34/36 Quai National, Tour Belle Rive 92800 Puteaux, France
Italy	COELTE (Costruzioni Elettromeccaniche Tiflotecnica per i non Vedenti) 24032 Calolziocorte (BG)
Netherlands	E.S.I (Efficiency Systems International bv), Postbus 69 2910 Ab Nieuwerkerk a/d Ijessel
Norway	Syberg & Syberg, Ostre Aker vei 215, Oslo 9
Spain	Eurotronica, Don Ramon de la Cruz 90, Madrid 6
Sweden	DBF Försäljningsaktiebolaget, Sandsborgsvägen 50, 122 33 Enskede
United Kingdom	SAGEM Communications Ltd., 11th Floor, Pembroke House, 44 Wellesley Road, Croydon, CRO 9WX
United States	Telesensory Systems Inc., 3408 Hillview Avenue, Palo Alto, CA 94304

(iii)   *Stiftung*   Stiftung Rehabilitation
        Rehabilitation   Postfach 101 409,
                                       6900 Heidelberg 1
                                       Federal Republic of Germany

(iv)   *SIGMA Electronic*   Sigma Electronic Systems Ltd
        Systems Ltd   Church Street
                                       Warnham
                                       Horsham RH12 30W
                                       United Kingdom

(v)   *Tele-ekonomi AB*   Tele-ekonomi AB
                                       Hardemogatan 1
                                       S-124 44 Bandhagen
                                       Sweden

(c) *Computer-aided translation of print to Braille*
     (i)   *Dotsys III*   Available from:
                                       Harvard-MIT Rehabilitation
                                          Engineering Center
                                       MIT Building 31-063
                                       Cambridge
                                       Massachusetts 02139
                                       United States
                                       (available, but unsupported)

                                       Improved version from:
                                       Atlanta Public Schools
                                       210 Pryor Street
                                       Atlanta
                                       Georgia 30303
                                       United States

                                       Dr D. Keeping
                                       University of Manitoba
                                       118c Engineering Building
                                       Winnipeg
                                       Manitoba R3T 2N2
                                       Canada

                                       Duxbury Systems Limited
                                       (see (ii) below)

     (ii)   *Duxbury Systems Inc.*   Duxbury Systems Inc.
                                       123 Lowell Drive
                                       Stow
                                       Massachusetts 01775
                                       United States

The following used the Duxbury Braille translator, November 1978:
                                       Canadian National Institute for
                                          the Blind
                                       1929 Bayview Avenue
                                       Toronto
                                       Ontario M4G 3E8
                                       Canada

Clovernook Home and Schools for
the Blind
7000 Hamilton Avenue
Cincinnati
Ohio 45231
United States

The National Braille Press Inc.
88 St Stephen Street
Boston
Massachusetts 02115
United States

Professional Service Center for
the Visually Handicapped
1700 West State Street
Janesville
Wisconsin 53545
United States

Royal New South Wales Institute for
Deaf and Blind Children
111-115 Chandos Street
St Leonards
Sydney
New South Wales 2065
Australia

Kurzweil Computer Products Inc.
264 Third Street
Cambridge
Massachusetts 02142
United States

Harrison Lions Club
c/o Jack Short
Arkansas Acceptance Corporation
P.O. Box 189
Harrison
Arkansas 72601
United States

(iii)   *University of*   Professor Dr Helmut Werner
        Münster   Rechenzentrum der Universität
                                     Münster
                                 4400 Münster
                                 Roxeler Strasse 60
                                 Federal Republic of Germany

(iv)   *Dutch Library for*   R. van Vliet
        the Blind   Nederlandsche Blindenbibliotheek
                                 Zilhtenburglaan 260
                                 2544 EB 's-Gravenhage
                                 Netherlands

(v)   *State Printing House*   Gunnar Reisler
        for the Blind   Statens Trykkeri for Blinde
        (Denmark)   Ronnegade 1
                                 2100 Copenhagen 0
                                 Denmark

Programme developed by   Jorgen Vinding
                                        Dansk Blindesamfund
                                        Randersgade 68
                                        2100 Copenhagen 0
                                        Denmark

(vi)   *Centre TOBIA*   Dr Monique Truquet
                                        Centre TOBIA
                                        Université Paul Sabatier
                                        118 route de Narbonne
                                        31077 Toulouse
                                        France

(vii)   *Laboratoire de*   J. M. Charpentier
        Recherche pour la   LRRPH
        Réinsertion   Conservatoire National des Arts et
        Professionnelle   Métiers
        des Handicapés   292 rue Saint-Martin
                                       75141 Paris Cedex 03
                                       France

(viii) *University of*   Dr P. A. Fortier
        Manitoba, Canada   University of Manitoba
                                       Department of French and Spanish
                                       Winnipeg
                                       Manitoba R3T 2N2
                                       Canada

                                       Dr D. Keeping
                                       University of Manitoba
                                       118c Engineering Building
                                       Winnipeg
                                       Manitoba R3T 2N2
                                       Canada

(ix)   *Applied Research*   Charlie Goh Sin Chan
        Corp./Singapore   Singapore Association for the Blind
        Assoc. for the   47 Toa Payoh Rise
        Blind   Singapore 11

(x)   *Tele-ekonomi AB/*   B. Hampshire
        Synskadades   Synskadades Riksförbund
        Riksförbund   122 88 Enskede
                                       Sweden

(xi)   *Subcommittee on*   Mr D. W. Croisdale (Chairman)
        Computerised Braille   Civil Service College
        Production and   11 Belgrave Road
        other Media   London SW1V 1RB
                                       United Kingdom

                                       Mr R. A. J. Gildea
                                       SIGCAPH
                                       The Mitre Corporation
                                       Box 208
                                       Bedford
                                       MA 01730
                                       United States

                                       Professor Dr H. Werner
                                       (see (iii) above)

(xii)   *Warwick Research*   Dr J. M. Gill
       Unit for the   WRUB
       Blind   University of Warwick
                         Coventry CV4 7AL
                         United Kingdom

(d) *Sequential Braille embossers*
    (i)   SAGEM   see (b) (ii) above.

    (ii)   *Triformation Systems Inc.*   see (b) (i) above.

    (iii)   *IBM*   IBM Corporation
                         Data Processing Division
                         1133 Westchester Avenue
                         White Plains
                         NY 10604
                         United States

(e) *Parallel embossers*
    (i)   *Marburg Automated*   see 2 (i) above
          Stereotype

    (ii)   *Triformation Systems Inc.*   see (b) (i).

(f) *Embossers under development*
    (i)   *SINTEF*   K. Grimnes
                         SINTEF
                         Aud. Reguleringsteknikk
                         N-7034 Trondheim-NTH
                         Norway

    (ii)   *Thiel GmbH*   Dipl. Phys. H.J. Thiel
                         D-6104 Jugenheim
                         Pauerweg 4
                         Postfach 88
                         Federal Republic of Germany

    (iii)   *Zoltan Braille embosser*   Trask Datasystem AB
                         Stockholmsvägen 34
                         182 74 Stocksund
                         Sweden

    (iv)   *L.-E. Andersson*   Lars-Eric Andersson
                         Nygatan 91 A
                         931 00 Skelleftea
                         Sweden

(g) *Post embossing equipment*
    (i)   *Bursters and*   BPC Business Forms Limited
          cutters   Whitehall Road
                         Leeds LS12 1BD
                         United Kingdom

                         Böhler and Weber KG
                         Maschinenfabrik
                         89 Augsburg
                         Haunsketter Strasse 12
                         Federal Republic of Germany
                         (Trade name: Böwe)

(ii)	*Hobson collator*	Hobson Designs Limited 337 High Road Ilford Essex United Kingdom

(iii)   *Spiral binding*

James Burn Bindings Limited
Douglas Road
Esher
Surrey KT10 8BD
United Kingdom

Spiral Binding Co. Inc.
2 Bridewell Place
Clifton
NJ 07014
United States

(iv)   *Velo-bind*

Fa. Gestetner GmbH
Postfach 500 460
8000 München 50
Federal Republic of Germany
or:

Gestetner Duplicators Limited
P.O. Box 23
Gestetner House
210 Euston Road
London NW1 2DA
United Kingdom

Special modification for Braille embossed paper available from:
Stiftung Rehabilitation
6900 Heidelberg 1
Postfach 101 409
Federal Republic of Germany

4. *Special Braille production equipment*
    (a) *Braille shorthand, stenography machines*

RNIB
(see 1(i))

Deutsche Blindenstudienanstalt
(see 1(ii))

Büromaschinen-Export GmbH
Friedrichstrasse 61–62
108 Berlin
German Democratic Republic

(b) *Simultaneous inkprint/Braille typewriters*
    (i)   *El-Op Brailler*

The Israel Electro-Optical Industry Limited
P.O. Box 1165
Rehovot
Israel

(ii)   *SP-200 inkprint/*
        Braille typewriter

Connecticut Technical Corp.
3000 Main Street
Hartford
CT 06120
United States

(iii)	*IBM 735 with braillomat tape embosser*	Dipl. Phys. H. J. Thiel (see 3(f) (ii) above)
(iv)	*Watari electric Braille typewriter*	Fuji Seisakusho Limited 7–14 Tsudahamano-cho Tokushima Japan

5. *Equipment for raised diagrams*
   (a) *Spur wheels*

RNIB (see 1(i))

Deutsche Blindenstudienanstalt (see 1(ii))

National Centre for the Blind Department of Social Welfare Government of India Dehra Dun India

(b) *Upward relief drawers*
   (i) *Leveau relief drawing board*

Union des Aveugles de Guerre 49 rue Blanche 75009 Paris France

(ii) *Upward relief drawer*

Blinden- und Sehschwachen-Verband Burgauenstrasse 9 7033 Leipzig German Democratic Republic

(i) *Upward relief drawer*

Deutsche Blindenstudienanstalt (see 1(ii))

(iv) *Raised line drawing kit*

Japan Braille Library 1–23–4 Takadanobaba Shinjuku-ku Tokyo 160 Japan

Instituut voor Perceptie Onderzoek Insulindelaan 2 Eindhoven The Netherlands

American Foundation for the Blind 15 West 16th Street New York NY 10011 United States

(v) *The sensory quill*

Texas Polytechnic and Research Institute 830 N.E. Loop 410 – Suite 210 San Antonio Texas 78209 United States (Att: Dr Traylor)

(c) *Masters for vacuum forming*

Nottingham Map-Making Kit
Blind Mobility Research Unit
Psychology Department
The University
Nottingham
United Kingdom

(d) *Photo-etching and screen printing*

Kissel and Wolf GmbH
D-6908 Wieslach
P.O. Box 1326
Federal Republic of Germany

Synskadades Riksförbund
(see 3c (x))

Appendix C

Sources of information relating to Braille

This appendix covers the main sources from which information relating to Braille can be obtained. It is divided into four main sections:

Bibliographies: contains bibliographies relating to Braille that have been published since 1970.

Conference reports: published reports or proceedings from the major conferences dealing entirely, or in part, with matters relating to Braille that have been held since 1970.

Journals: the major journals published dealing specifically with blindness or visual impairment and which also include articles relating to Braille.

Registers and catalogues.

Bibliographies

GILL, J. M. Bibliography on Braille Automation and Related Research. *Braille Research Newsletter*, No. 7, May 1978.

LORIMER, P. M. *The Braille Code and the Teaching of Braille Reading and Writing: An Annotated Bibliography.* Research Centre for the Education of the Visually Handicapped, Faculty of Education, University of Birmingham, United Kingdom. 1978.

Research Centre for the Education of the Visually Handicapped. Educational Research Abstracts. Occasional research abstracts compiled and sent out by RCEVH (see Appendix D).

SYNDOC. The Swedish Institute for the Handicapped. This is a data base containing approximately 1,400 documents. Each document is assigned a key or search word selected from a list of approximately 100 such words. In 1979, the system was being developed so as to enable its regular up-dating—every other month—and to permit listings to be given out more often. It will also be possible to order specific searches through the data base. For further information contact: The Library, The Swedish Institute for the Handicapped, 161 25 Bromma 1, Sweden.

GILL, J. M. Tactual Mapping: Bibliography. *AFB Research Bulletin* (New York, American Foundation for the Blind), No. 29, 1974, p. 64-80.

ÖSTBERG, A.-M.; LINDQVIST, B. *Learning Problems in Connection with Information Media for the Visually Handicapped—A Selected Bibliography.* Report No. 11, 1970. Project: PUSS III. Uppsala University, Pedagogoska Institutionen.

Conference reports

Tactile Displays Conference.
IEEE Transactions MMS-11, 1970, 1. Special Issue. 122 p.

European Conference on Educational Research for the Visually Handicapped.
Lindqvist, B. and Trowald, N. (eds.) 1972.
Project: PUSS VIII. Report No. 31. 90 p.

Fifth Quinquennial Conference of the International Council for the Education of Blind Youth.
(Motto: New Subjects, New Methods and New Pupils in the Education of the Visually Handicapped).
Madrid, 25 July – 2 August, 1972.

The Leonard Conference on Research into Visual Handicap.
Girton College, Cambridge University. 1972.
Southern Regional Association for the Blind, 32 Old Queen Street, London, SW1H 9HP. (Conference Report No. 62).

European Braille Conference. Oslo, 26–28 September 1973.
European Regional Committee of the WCWB and Norges Blindeforbund.

Computerised Braille Production.
Proceedings of the International Workshop in Münster, March 1973.
Gildea, R.A.J., Hübner, G. and Werner, H.
No. 9, Dec. 1974. Rechenzentrum: Universität Münster.
Reprinted as: Proceedings of the Workshop 'Towards the Communality of Algorithms Among Braille Transcription Systems for Multilingual Usage'.
SIGCAPH Newsletter, No. 15, March 1975.

Proceedings of the World Assembly of the World Council for the Welfare of the Blind.
Sao Paulo, Brazil. 7–16 August 1974.
Available from: WCWB, 58 avenue Bosquet, 75007, Paris, France.

The Louis Braille British Conference on Research into Reading and Listening by the Visually Handicapped.
Girton College, Cambridge University. 1975.
Southern Regional Association for the Blind. (See Ref. 4.)
Conference Report No. 66.

On Creating an International Information System on Visual Impairment and Blindness.
Report of a Seminar held during the European Technical Conference of the E.R.C. of the WCWB.
12 April 1977. London.
Gill, J. M. and Clark, L. L.
Warwick Research Unit for the Blind. April 1977.

Conference on Technical Aids for the Blind.
London. April 1977. Technical Aids Committee for the European Regional Council.
Dansk Blindesamfund. Copenhagen, 1977.

Sixth Quinquennial Conference of International Council of Education of the Visually Handicapped. 1977, August, Paris. (In preparation.)

European Conference of Directors of Braille Printing Houses and Braille Libraries. Madrid, 11–13 April 1978.
European Regional Committee of WCWB, Organizacion Nacional de Ciegos, C/Jose Ortega y Gasset 18, Madrid 6, Spain.

Computerized Braille Production — Today. Tomorrow. 30 May–1 June 1979. Committee on Cultural Affairs, WCWB, Royal National Institute for the Blind, 224 Great Portland Street, London W1N 6AA.

Journals

Journal of Visual Impairment and Blindness
ISSN: 0145 482x.
Editors: Mulholland, M. E., Smith, P. S., Clark, L. L.
Publisher: American Foundation for the Blind.
Publisher's address: 15 West 16th St., New York, New York 10011, United States.
Tel: (212) 924 0420.
Languages of publication: English.
Languages of abstracts: English.
Indexed and/or abstracted in: Current Contents, Exceptional Child Education Abstracts, Excerpta Medica, Language and Language Behaviour Abstracts, Abstracts for Social Workers, Rehabilitation Literature, Psychological Abstracts, Health & Medical Care Services Review, Blindness, Visual Impairment, Deal-Blindness.
Media: Inkprint, Braille, Record.
Frequency of Publication: 10 times per year.
Annual cost: US$ 11. Additional foreign postage $ 1.50.
Coverage: Interdisciplinary journal of record for practitioners and researchers professionally concerned with blind and visually impaired persons. Major articles on research and practice aspects of dealing with vision impairment (does not deal with prevention); brief reports of new practice techniques research projects; news; literature sections; reviews.
Source of information: J. M. Gill, *International Register of Research on Blindness and Visual Impairment*, Warwick Research Unit for the Blind, 1977.

Education of the Visually Handicapped
Editor: Walker, Dr. D. L.
Publisher: Association for the Education of the Visually Handicapped.
Publisher's address: 4th Floor, 919 Walnut Street Philadelphia, Pennsylvania 19107, United States.
Tel: (215) WA 3 7555.
Languages of publication: English.
Languages of abstracts: English.
Abstracted by: Psychological Abstracts, Exceptional Child Education Abstracts.
Media: Inkprint, Braille.
Frequency of publication: Quarterly.
Coverage: Articles of interest to educators of visually handicapped children, chiefly reports of research or of procedural innovations.
Source of information: J. M. Gill, *International Register of Research on Blindness and Visual Impairment*, Warwick Research Unit for the Blind, 1977.

Braille Research Newsletter
Editors: Gill, Dr. J. M. and Clark, L. L.
Publisher: Warwick Research Unit for the Blind.
Publisher's address: University of Warwick, Coventry CV4 7AL, United Kingdom.
Tel: 0203 24011.
Languages of publication: English.
Frequency of publication: Irregular.
Annual cost: Free to contributors.
Coverage: Research and development involving Braille production, and studies on the Braille code.
Source of information: J. M. Gill, *International Register of Research on Blindness and Visual Impairment*, Warwick Research Unit for the Blind, 1977.

Educator
Editor: Heisler, W. T.
Publisher: Perkins School for the Blind.
Publisher's address: 175 North Beacon St., Watertown, Massachusetts 02172, United States.
Tel: (617) 924 3434.
Languages of publication: English, Spanish.
Languages of abstracts: English, Spanish.
Media: Inkprint, Braille.
Frequency of publication: twice yearly.
Annual cost: US$3 per quinquennium or as an accompaniment to membership in the International Council for the Education of the Visually Handicapped.
Coverage: This is the organ of the International Council for the Education of the Visually Handicapped (ICEVH) and contains articles primarily dealing with educational programmes, techniques, research and events in the field of the education of the visually handicapped. An effort is made to utilize a theme for each issue. Contributors include teachers of the visually handicapped, research workers, administrators of programmes, college instructors and others affiliated in any way with the overall programme dealing with the education of visually handicapped children and youth.
Source of information: J. M. Gill, *International Register of Research on Blindness and Visual Impairment*, Warwick Research Unit for the Blind, 1977.

Registers and catalogues

International Register of Research on Blindness and Visual Impairment

This register, which is compiled by the Warwick Research Unit for the Blind in collaboration with the American Foundation for the Blind, is divided into three sections:
   (i) List of projects on non-medical research and innovative practice for the blind and visually impaired.
   (ii) List of the main organizations, in each country, of and for the blind and visually impaired, which are likely to be of interest to those involved in research and innovative practice.
   (iii) List of sources of information including periodicals, abstract journals, information services and reference works.
   The Register is held in machine-readable form to facilitate updating and to enable the fast production of versions in grade I and grade 2 Braille.
   At the present time (1980) the language of the Register is English only since the cost of translation into other languages is prohibitive. There is interest, however, on the part of the Warwick Research Unit for the Blind (WRUB) in co-operating with other organizations to make the Register available in other languages.
   From an analysis of the subject index to section (i) there are sixty-one people listed under the heading 'Braille'. Of these, by far the greatest number is engaged in technological aspects; of these sixty-one, forty-eight are also listed under 'Computers', or 'Devices and Equipment', or 'Displays and Display Systems', or 'Embossing Machines and Systems'.
   The only other significant grouping of Braille researchers is in the area of psychological/educational investigations; of the sixty-one listed under 'Braille', ten are also listed under 'Education' or 'Test and Measurements' or 'Children' or 'Perception/Recognition' or 'Reading and Reading Machines'.

International Guide to Aids and Appliances for Blind and Visually Impaired Persons

This catalogue includes aids and equipment relating to Braille under the following headings:
   Braille Equipment
   Braille Writing Aids
   Braille Instruction
   Braille Paper, Notebooks, Binders, Filing Aids.
   The catalogue is available from the American Foundation for the Blind, Inc., 15 West 16th Street, New York NY10011, United States.

Appendix D

Research centres

This appendix gives names and address of the main established centres carrying out research in the area of visual handicap and blindness. Those projects relating to Braille are described briefly.

1. *American Printing House for the Blind: Department of Educational Research*
   Address: 839 Frankfort Avenue, P.O. 6085, Louisville, Kentucky 40206, United States.
   General Manager: Dr Carson Y. Nolan.
   General description: Current activities at APH includes basic research in tactile perception and materials development in the areas of social studies, sciences, listening comprehension, auditory and oral language development, recorded reference works, indexing systems for recording, and educational measurement. Research and development staff[1] consists of six senior researchers, four research assistants, an educational aids technician and secretarial support.
   Projects relating to Braille: 'Beginning Braille Reading Series': A three-year project, initiated in 1975, to develop a set of Braille reading materials designed to overcome or minimize many of the problems encountered by children who must learn to read using the Braille code has been carried out. Plans were made to continue the field evaluation and revisions of the pre-primer, primer, first, second and third grade materials during 1979.

2. *Baruch Computer Research Center for the Visually Impaired*
   Address: Computer Center for the Visually. Impaired Baruch College/CUNY, 17 Lexington Avenue, Box 264, New York 10010, United States.
   Associate director: Ms Randi Baker.
   Projects relating to Braille: (1) National sample survey of Braille and large print reading public in the United States (in collaboration with AFB), (2) Computerized production of tactile graphics, (3) Production of private information (e.g., bank statements) in Braille and (4) Production of abstracts of academic publications in Braille.
   Source of information: L. L. Clark, 'Baruch Computer Center for the Visually Impaired', *Braille Research Newsletter*, No. 8, September 1978, p. 2–9.

3. *Laboratoire de Recherche pour la Recherche pour la Réinsertion des Handicapés*
   Address: Conservatoire National des Arts et Métiers, 2 rue Conté, 75003 Paris, France.
   Director: Professor L. Avan.
   Projects relating to Braille: Development of automated systems for producing literary text, music and mathematics in Braille.
   Source of information: J. M. Gill, *International Register of Research on Blindness and Visual Impairment*, Warwick Research Unit for the Blind, 1977.
   Criterion-referenced tests for beginning Braille readers: A set of criterion-referenced tests to accompany the

1. 1977 figures.

'Beginning Braille Reading Series' was developed during 1978. Data from field trials of the items will be analysed, final items selected and final editions of the tests prepared for production, during the period 1979–81.

Tactile display kit: Development of a tactile display kit and manual for teachers to show them how to apply the results of research to train students to read tactile maps and diagrams more effectively as well as providing information for design of their own tactile graphics.

Source of information: Personal communication from Dr Hilda Caton, 15 November, 1978.

Department of Educational Research: Report on Research and Development Activities, Fiscal 1978. American Printing House for the Blind.

4. *NAB Louis Braille Memorial Research Centre*

Address: c/o The Workshop for the Blind, 2nd Floor, Prabhadevi, Bombay 400 025, India.

Chairman: Prof. M. Y. Bhide.

Activities relating to Braille: Braille code for signs and symbols for teaching new maths. Manufacture and distribution of styli. Cell for repair and service of Braille writers. A research study concerning Braille reading techniques. Developing abbreviations and contractions in Bharati Braille.

Source of information: Personal communication from Prof. M. Y. Bhide, 10 October 1978.

5. *Perceptual Alternatives Laboratory.*

Address: 358 Life Sciences Building, University of Louisville, Louisville, Kentucky 40208, United States.

Director: Dr Emerson Foulke.

Projects relating to Braille: Development of computer-assisted Braille production systems.

Source of information: J. M. Gill, *International Register of Research on Blindness and Visual Impairment*, Warwick Research Unit for the Blind, 1977.

6. *Research Centre for the Education of the Visually Handicapped*

Address: University of Birmingham, Faculty of Education, Selly Wick House, 59 Selly Wick Road, Birmingham, B29 7JF, United Kingdom.

Director: Dr Michael J. Tobin.

Projects relating to Braille: 'Improving Efficiency in Braille Reading': (i) A series of controlled experiments of techniques and materials for raising reading efficiency was conducted during 1976 and 1977. These are being used to prepare a teachers' handbook; it is intended to up-date this publication in due course in the light of the results of further trials of the procedures. (ii) A series of investigations on the effect on reading time of simpler Braille codes which take up more space.

Source of information: RCEVH Director's Eighth Report, December 1977.

7. *TOBIA (Transcription par ordinateur Braille intégral et abrégé)*

Address: Université Paul Sabatier, 118 route de Narbonne, 31077 Toulouse Cedex, France.

Director: Monique Truquet.

Activities relating to Braille: The centre functions as a service centre open to anyone wanting Braille documents, such as school books, novels, special documents, material for exams, bank statements, etc. A computer-assisted system is used which utilizes translation programmes developed at TOBIA. Some work on developing a translation programme for Spanish has been carried out but this was halted as the Spanish Braille system is being changed. Computer-assisted transcription of mathematics, science, and music texts is being worked on.

Source of information: Personal communication from Monique Truquet, 8 November 1978.

8. *School of Education, Uppsala University*

Address: School of Education, Uppsala University, Box 2109, Avd. Sysslomansgatan, 750 02 Uppsala, Sweden.

Director: Dr Nils Trowald.

General description: Starting in 1969, the School of Education at Uppsala has conducted a major research project concerning the study situation for the visually handicapped. This project, called PUSS (Educational Investigations Concerning the Study Situation of the Visually Handicapped), covered a wide range and attempted to analyse numerous factors connected with the study and learning situation of the visually handicapped. The PUSS project was concluded in 1975 in accordance with the original plans. In 1976 a new plan was developed dealing with a further project, FOUKUS (Research and Development Work Concerning Teaching Methods for the Visually Handicapped). A number of the projects within FOUKUS finished in 1979. In 1979, the continuation of research into the visually handicapped at Uppsala was uncertain.

Projects relating to Braille: By means of investigations and methodic developmental work concerning in particular the reading media of talking books, Braille, the Optacon and large-type, the project seeks to optimize the reading options available to the visually handicapped.

Publications: More than seventy reports have been published by the School of Education, over twenty from the PUSS project and five from FOUKUS. Many of these relate to Braille and other reading media. A full list of publications is given at the end of each published report.

Source of information: Nils Trowald, *Rapport nr 59, 1976. Projektet FOUKUS: I. En presentation av fortsättningen pa synforskningsprojektet PUSS.*

3. *Warwick Research Unit for the Blind* (WRUB)

Address: University of Warwick, Coventry CV4 7AL, United Kingdom.

Director: Dr John M. Gill.

General description: WRUB consists of four staff members — Dr Gill, a research assistant, plus two secretaries. The main activities of the research centre concern the development of computer-assisted Braille production and the collection, analysis and dissemination of information relating to research into blindness and visual handicap.

Projects relating to Braille: Design and evaluation of computer-based systems for automatically producing contracted Braille from text already in digital form. The automated production of bank statements in Braille. Development of an automated current alerting system for blind psychologists. A study of the Braille code involving an analysis of the frequency of use of contractions.

Project to evolve a methodology for the design of a high quality Braille translation programme, appropriate for a wide range of Braille codes.

Publications: The Warwick Research Unit for the Blind, in co-operation with the American Foundation for the Blind, is responsible for publishing the *International Register of Research on Blindness and Visual Impairment* (see Appendix C). The Unit has also published over forty articles, mainly relating to tactual maps and computer-aided Braille production.

Appendix E

Braille recorders:
description and specifications

DIGICASSETTE

Manufacturer:	Electronique Linguistique Informatique Appliquées 'Elfina'
	3 bis, rue Le Corbusier – SILIC 231
	94528 Rungis Cedex
	France
Dimensions:	8 × 9 × 2 inches
Weight:	4 lb.

Features: '7-key electric keyboard (one key for each Braille dot and one key for space). Typing is fast and silent. Reading is by 12 character lines, which follow each other at rate controlled by reader.

'One standard C-90 cassette contains 300,000 Braille characters (150,000 on each track) equivalent to a 220 page pocket book or 6 Braille volumes.

'The Braille recorder is connectable to various electronic pocket or desk calculators. All operations and mathematical functions are immediately available in Braille.

'A microphone and a loudspeaker allow the recorder to be used as an ordinary cassette sound recorder.

'A switch allows change immediately from sound to Braille (or the reverse) on same tape'.

An interface is available which 'converts Braille characters for read/write operations to and from the Braille recorder into an asynchronous stream of serial characters which conforms to the CCITT V-24 recommendations'.

Price:	Approximately 1,800 French francs ($410)
Source of information:	Manufacturer's brochures.

BRAILLOCORD

Manufacturer:	ALD Electronic GmbH Berlin
	Wilhelm von Siemens Strasse 16–18
	D-100 West Berlin 48
Dimensions:	35 × 14 × 33 cm. (14 × 5.5 × 13 inches)
Weight:	About 7 kg. (15.4 lbs.)

Features: 'This Braille reading and writing system receives and sends out information in a format of 32 lines of 32 characters each. This is approximately the information content of a typical page of Braille. The information is stored in an ordinary C-60 or C-90 magnetic tape cassette, the same as used in audio applications in the common cassette recorder. Using one C-90 compact cassette, up to 400 pages of text can be stored and retrieved. Playback of Braille text occurs without unwanted pauses on an electromechanical Braille line, a line at a time, from the electronic buffer store, with the operation of a single key. Reading can be done at a rate selected by the individual reader, in the manner he is accustomed to in reading ordinary Braille pages. Text can be in contracted or uncontracted Braille code.'

Price:	DM.8,450 ($3,500)
Source of information:	'The BRS 76 Braillocord System.' *Braille Research Newsletter.* (Eds. Gill and Clark.) No. 6, October 1977. Warwick Research Unit for the Blind. University of Warwick, Coventry CV4 7AL, United Kingdom. (Translated from German by L. L. Clark.)

BRAILLEX

Manufacturer:	Papenmeier Elektro-Technik Postfach 1620 D-5840 Schwerte 1 Federal Republic of Germany
Dimensions:	40 × 45 × 15 cm. (15.8 × 17.7 × 5.9 inches)
Weight:	16 kg.
Features:	'Storage of any information and sequencing symbols, catch words for example, on a standard ready-to-use magnetic tape cassette. 'Compact digital storage of Braille on magnetic tape. 'Input and output of information in terms of – spoken language – Braille – combination spoken language and Braille 'Quick access to programmed information from magnetic tape cassettes. 'Input and programming of user's information. 'Short access time (microprocessor-based construction permits automatic search for letter strings at about 500 words per second). '. . . a C-60 cassette—fully programmed—(on both tracks) stores a volume of about 720,000 characters or figures. 'Minimized keyboard operations through built-in highly integrated electronics with microprocessor serving as the central unit.'
Price:	DM.10,000 ($4,750)
Source of information:	Manufacturer's brochure and F. H. Papenmeier, 'The BRAILLEX system', *Braille Research Newsletter*, No. 7, March 1978. (Eds. Gill and Clark.) Warwick Research Unit for the Blind, Coventry CV4 7AL, United Kingdom.

VERSABRAILLE

Manufacturer:	Telesensory Systems Inc. 3408 Hillview Avenue P.O. Box 10099 Palo Alto California 94304 United States
Dimensions:	23 × 35.5 × 9.5 cm. (9 × 14 × 3.175 inches)
Weight:	4.5 kg. (10 lb.)
Features:	'Compact, operates on rechargeable batteries (charger included). 'Complete 6-key Braille writing capability. 'Advanced, electronically activated Braille cells. 'Braille cell dimension identical to standard Braille. 'Solid state buffer memory with 1,000 character storage. 'Full page (1,000 character) immediate editing capability.

'Computer grade digital electronic tape transport.
'Braille reading on a 20 cell line.
'Audio record and playback facility.
'Input/output connector for future attachment of accessories.
'Microcomputer-controlled automatic location of stored information by topic — eliminates need for tape footage counter.
'Microcomputer controlled display — prevents splitting of words at end of 20-character line.'

Price:	approximately $4,500 (1980)
Source of information:	TSI Progress Report. September 1978.

BRAILINK

Manufacturer:	Clark & Smith International Limited Melbourne House Melbourne Road Wallington Surrey United Kingdom
Dimensions:	46 × 33 × 15 cm.
Weight:	–
Features:	Brailink is a soft copy Braille terminal providing immediate data access facilities. It is a direct alternative to teletype or similar access terminal. It allows a blind operator full control over interrogation of the computer and data output. The unit contains a keyboard for data entry, a line of Braille cells 48 characters long, a buffer memory which holds two current half lines with a maximum of 96 characters, one of the half lines is displayed in Braille. There is interface for data tape deck facilities. The Brailink comes complete with a data recorder using a four track cassette, density 1,600 bytes per inch (bpi)
Price:	£3,785 ($7,800) Cost of both units supplied together.
Source of information:	Personal communication, 9 October 1978. Mr W. S. Hedges, Director, Clark & Smith.

BD-80

Manufacturer:	Dipl. Ing. K-P Schönherr Medizin- u. Rehabilitationstechnik Schloss Solitude Hans 3 D-700 Stuttgart 1
Dimensions:	50 × 24 × 8 cm.
Weight:	–
Features:	The BD-80 achieves complete Braille representation of alpha numerical data from electric typewriters, text automats and CRT terminals. The information is displayed by 80 Braille modules, 8 dots each, arranged in 2 rows of 40 modules. Lower and upper case letters are distinguished by dot 7. Actual position of ball printing head of typewriter or cursor of CRT terminal is represented by dot 8. The BD-80, containing a microprocessor, may easily be adapted to various needs. Keyboards for ASC11 code or 6 and 8 dot Braille, mass storage facilities (floppy disk or cassette) and the Braille reading/writing device BRAILLOCORD BRS 76 are available. A range of Braille displays can be purchased from Schönherr.

Standard units are as follows:
40 character modules of 8 dots
36 character modules of 6 dots
32 character modules of 6 dots
16 character modules of 4 dots
Single character modules (see plate 1) can also be purchased.

Price: BD-80 Unit: DM9,000 (approx. $4,800)
1 line of 40 Braille modules of 8 dots cost:
DM.3,500 (including motherboard and plugs).

*Source of
information:*   Manufacturer's brochure.

Appendix F

The 'U' and Nemeth systems for representing mathematics and science in Braille

I have chosen these two Braille notation systems for further comparison as they represent two quite different approaches to the representation of mathematics and science in Braille. Furthermore, the Nemeth system is used throughout North America and has been used as a basis for systems in other countries, e.g. the Bharati Braille code for mathematics in India. Also, the 'U' notation is the system being developed under the auspices of WCWB's Sub-committee on Mathematical and Science Notation. Thus, both these systems have, albeit potentially in the case of the latter, a usage which goes beyond the boundaries of a single country.

The 'U' notation is being based on a theoretical foundation currently under development by a group working in the Soviet Union and a Spanish group is establishing the Braille presentations with the help of comments and criticisms which they are collecting about their proposals from all WCWB member countries. It is hoped, therefore, that the 'U' notation will eventually be adopted by the majority of countries in Europe, including the Soviet Union, at least. It is, however, unlikely that North America or other countries which are already using the Nemeth code will replace this in favour of another system.

General principles

Nemeth Code:[1] Perhaps the most fundamental feature of this code is its attempt to 'convey as accurate an impression as is possible to the Braille reader of the corresponding printed text . . .'. Of course, the many hundreds of arbitary signs which are used in the inkprint mathematical and science notation cannot be directly represented by the sixty-three Braille characters and thus a system of 'Braille indicators' are used.

These Braille indicators do not correspond to any sign in inkprint. However, they have the power of importing meaning to the Braille symbols with which they are associated. By their use it is possible to represent the numerous type forms and alphabets used in inkprint and to convey the 'two-dimensional' information contained in inkprint through the medium of the Braille system whose nature is essentially 'one-dimensional'.

'U' Notation:[2] In a short report following the International Meeting on the Unification of Braille Mathematics and Science Notation held in Moscow in 1976 some general principles were recommended for the development of Braille mathematics and science notation and these have been employed in the development of the 'U' system. These are as follows:

1. The original Braille signs for letters should be preserved.
2. Provision should be made for representing a broader range of mathematics and science texts as the needs arise.
3. Unless there are strong reasons against it, every inkprint symbol should have only one Braille counterpart, different inkprint symbols having different Braille counterparts.
4. The system should be uniform at all educational levels.
5. The principle of economy should be observed where it does not conflict with clarity of the expression.
6. Embossed diagrams and tables should be easily understood by touch.

The major feature in which the two systems under consideration differ is with regard to principle number 5 above. Since the Nemeth code strives to give the reader an accurate impression of what the inkprint text looks like, this can often mean that Nemeth representations are considerably more space consuming than the equivalent representation in the 'U' notation. This and other differences are illustrated by some examples given below.

Arabic numerals

Both the Nemeth code and the 'U' notation use the standard number sign ⠒ However, the Nemeth code then uses the letter signs 'j' and 'a' to 'i' but occupy the lower half of the cell. The 'U' notation represents these numerals in the same way as literary Braille codes. Thus:

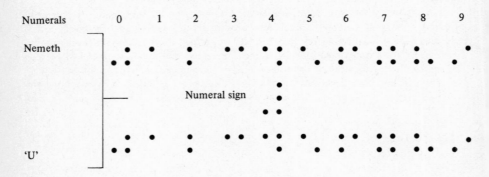

Letters of different alphabets

Here the two systems use somewhat similar approaches, i.e. each use the original Braille signs for the letters but these are preceded by one or more signs to indicate what sort of letter they are. The Nemeth code, however, uses a separate sign for each parameter, e.g. alphabetic indicators, capitalization indicators, type-form indicators, and so on. The 'U' notation, on the other hand, has Braille indicators which impart information about more than one parameter, e.g. Latin capital letter, Greek capital letter are indicated by a single, but different, character before the actual letter character itself. Thus:

Nemeth Braille indicators

English letter	German letter	Greek letter *

Capitalization	Italics *	*Rules govern how these indicators are used so that their meaning is unambiguous.

'U' notation

Latin letter, small	Latin letter, capital	Greek letter, small

Greek letter, capital	German letter, small	German letter, capital

Italics, all letters

Signs of operation

These follow basically similar principles, at least at a simple level. However, Nemeth code's principle of following the inkprint layout means that a space is used before and after the 'equals' sign and this makes the expression longer.

	Plus +	Minus −	Multiplication ×	Divided by ÷	Equals =
Nemeth					
'U'					

Example:

$$Ax + Bx + C = x(A + B) + C$$

Nemeth

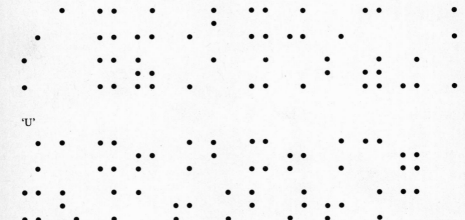

'U'

Functions

The approach of the two systems with regard to functions is totally different. The Nemeth code uses a direct transcription of the inkprint abbreviation in Braille, whereas the 'U' notation uses a special function sign (⠐) plus one or two other signs in association with it. With the Nemeth code spaces are also usually used after each function name so that these expressions can be very much longer than the equivalent in 'U' notation.

	Nemeth	'U'
Logarithm (log)		
Antilogarithm (antilog)		
Sine (sin)		
Cosine (cos)		
Tangent (tan)		